PREVENTING BULLYING IN SCHOOLS

PREVENTING BULLYING IN SCHOOLS

A Guide for Teachers and Other Professionals

Chris Lee

P·CP

Paul Chapman Publishing

Paul Chapman Publishing
A SAGE Publications Company
1 Oliver's Yard
55 City Road
London EC1Y 1SP

SAGE Publications Inc.
2455 Teller Road
Thousand Oaks, California 91320

SAGE Publications India Pvt Ltd
B-42, Panchsheel Enclave
Post Box 4109
New Delhi 110 017

Library of Congress Control Number: 2004090285

A catalogue record for this book is available from the British Library

ISBN 0 7619 4471 0
ISBN 0 7619 4472 9 (pbk)

Typeset by Pantek Arts Ltd, Maidstone, Kent
Printed in Great Britain by The Cromwell Press, Trowbridge, Wilts

CONTENTS

TABLES

AUTHOR BIOGRAPHY

Dr Chris Lee is a Principal Lecturer at the University of Plymouth where he works mainly with teachers researching their own practice and he also is Director in the MA (Education) programme. His main lecturing and research foci are bullying and behaviour management. Prior to his role as a lecturer he taught in both secondary and special education.

ACKNOWLEDGEMENTS

I am indebted to all those who have supported me, especially Lizzie, Nick and Ben. I should like to dedicate the book to Graham and Tom – both missed so much and both so influential in their own ways. Their wisdom and their smiles have been a powerful force.

CHAPTER 1

What this Book Will Do for You

This chapter sets the tone for the book both in style and content. It opens with an outline of the key principles that are central to the book, including that the most effective anti-bullying approaches and policies are whole-school issues. The book is full of activities which raise awareness and inform practice, and this chapter contains an outline of those activities that provide a first reference point for staff addressing bullying. Through the first activity, staff are invited to appraise the current standing of their own school on the bullying issue.

This book is designed to help all staff in schools prevent one of the major impediments to their attempts to raise standards and improve schools, and that is the issue of bullying amongst pupils. The book highlights and unravels some of the complexities of bullying and provides ideas and practical solutions to the problem of writing policy and realizing its aspirations. It has been designed and written for teachers, teaching assistants, student teachers and other educational professionals in schools who are the creators of that policy and who also are responsible for its implementation. It aims to raise awareness and develop effective policy and practice in preventing bullying by combining theory, research and experience of working in schools with a number of practical exercises which have been fine-tuned through my work with adults and children in schools. The activities included in the book provide the necessary elements of an anti-bullying policy based on effective practice.

The contents of the book are designed to:

- increase awareness and understanding of bullying;

- provide practical ideas that challenge assumptions, inspire discussion and support anti-bullying strategies undertaken in classrooms and around schools;

- inform the development of anti-bullying policies and inform practice that seeks to prevent bullying.

It offers ideas for those who work in schools and have already addressed bullying, as well as those who have yet to develop effective policy and practice in the area. With the focus on prevention it provides education professionals with opportunities to engage in activities and ideas whose effectiveness may not be measurable, since it would be impossible to quantify events that did not take place because they were prevented! It is not intended that acting upon ideas generated by this book will provide an instant set of solutions to bullying in schools – too many ideas are foisted upon professionals with an attached implication of 'do this and you will be doing the right thing and the problem will be resolved'. This book is about professionals exploring ways forward, providing structures, systems, policies, practices and, most important of all, understanding of a highly complex issue. First, let us consider what prevention involves.

Prevention and Principles

Prevention comprises:

- collaboration between all parties, rather than the assumption that it is one person's responsibility to ensure reconciliation, improved behaviour or, at least, an end to the bullying;

- regarding parents and caregivers as key players;

- clarity and consistency of procedures and interventions that recognize the difference that schools can make;

- empowering pupils to take responsibility for changing and maintaining their behaviour and influencing the behaviour of others;

- early intervention at the first signs of problems occurring within a relationship.

The contents of the book are based on many years and forms of research into pupils', teachers' and parents' experiences and perceptions of bullying, and I am also indebted to those who have joined me on professional development days and higher degree courses that have addressed the subject. Throughout the book theory, research and practice come together and are integrated with a view to enhancing understanding of bullying and providing staff with greater knowledge and expertise. All too often those charged with writing policies on bullying do so in isolation and are the sole arbiters of content with little ownership or knowledge existing beyond the writer. Using this book provides opportunities for staff and children to work on policy generation together, with the result that it is known, understood, agreed, owned and used by all.

The ideas within are not offered as a medicine which, when taken, alleviates symptoms or completely eradicates disease, but as ways of addressing the problem of bullying in schools in an open and direct way. Included in the principles that inform what follows are my beliefs that:

1 *Bullying is a whole-school matter.* Any anti-bullying approach should step beyond those pupils who are directly involved. Everyone has a part to play in countering bullying in schools, and addressing it is an opportunity to review the values that the school holds as central. A recent Office for Standards in Education (OFSTED) report, HMI 465 (OFSTED, 2003), linked schools that were successful in tackling bullying with consultation with pupils and observed that the schools found that active involvement of pupils arising from consultation was a key component in any preventative approach.

2 *A single incident is one too many.* Numerous researchers and writers have tried to quantify the extent of the bullying problem and have focused on measuring how many children are bullies or being bullied. Indeed, there will be limited reference to statistics that help to illustrate points in this book as they provide relevant data. However, it is essential to note that measuring levels of bullying may help to monitor the effectiveness of a policy, but bullying is a qualitative experience and just one incident can have a major impact on a child, those who know about it and the school itself.

3 *The importance of openness and transparency.* Being open and addressing the issue of bullying directly, in an informed and imaginative way, is preferable to perceiving it as something that only affects a few pupils and is, therefore, a background matter, a problem that is of little consequence. Bullying is not a topic that is side-lined into an occasional lesson or addressed through an occasional assembly. It is about teaching and learning. Pupils being bullied are not likely to achieve their full potential, nor will those who live in fear of bullying, nor will observers or bystanders unless the problem is resolved. Even perpetrators may achieve more academically with a positive deployment of their energies.

4 *A policy is more than a written document.* One of the benefits of the relatively recent interest in bullying in schools has been the encouragement that pupils often receive to speak openly about it and not consider it a secretive matter. However, with more open approaches, there comes a demand that action be taken, be seen to be taken and that schools are now required to have specific anti-bullying policies in place. Reducing bullying is so much more than the writing of a policy. It requires changes in attitudes and behaviours of staff who can provide a negative model by using aggression and inappropriate power and permit bullying by not intervening. Any written statement in the form of a policy contains statements that reflect more than the management of an anti-social behaviour; they mirror the values that underpin the school and all those who work in it. It is a *live* dynamic document – one which should be referred to, written on, questioned and revised. Unfortunately, schools are compelled to address such a range of issues that policies are all too often perceived as documents not manifestations of good practice.

The Structure of the Book and How to Use It

There are six chapters:

1 *What this book will do for you.* This sets the scene on what has informed this book, where attempts to create bully-free classrooms and schools have reached and what this book offers for those on that journey.

2 *How do we know when it is bullying?* Most anti-bullying policies open with a definition in an attempt to provide focus and to distinguish between bullying and other forms of aggression. Included here are a number of ideas on generating definitions, how problematic any definition can be and how to explore meaning as part of policy generation.

3 *Who are involved in bullying?* This chapter is a look at the traditional idea that bullies and victims are the involved group and provides helpful insights and advice. It then moves on to suggest that it is the bystander that has much to offer and that this term applies to pupils, staff and parents.

4 *What is needed in an anti-bullying policy.* This is an examination of the process of developing a policy as well as suggestions as to what a policy might contain.

5 *What might be put in place.* This is an account of a number of ways in which bullying can be countered and includes ways in which approaches may be introduced into the school.

6 *How to move your school forward.* This is a summary of the main themes, and some pointers towards the future.

Within each chapter is a *discussion* of the main issues that include advice for professionals, areas of debate and rationales for ideas, plus *findings* from professional development projects and research undertaken in schools and enhanced by a variety of tables that illustrate ideas and promote discussion. In addition, there are the *activities* for staff and pupils that inform professional development, and exercises that raise awareness and understanding in the classroom and beyond. These activities state whether they are designed for staff, pupils or both, but can be adapted to your own specific context. You will find it useful to appoint a co-ordinator to facilitate organization, discussion and decisions reached, but they do not have to be the policy-writer or the resident 'anti-bullying expert', indeed that is not a helpful model. Sharing the task of co-ordinating activities mirrors the model that we *all* have a responsibility to make a difference, not foist the role on the resident expert. If we are looking for experts, look no further than the pupil who gets called names all day long, or has his or her possessions taken or is socially ostracized, or all of these. They are the experts.

The Activities

Prior to undertaking any activity, staff involved in developing an anti-bullying policy and in tacking bullying should refer to the Index of Activities in the book (page 5) and select the activities that would form a professional development programme that addresses areas that require more awareness and enhanced practice. Completion of the activities will lead to completion of an anti-bullying policy and so much more than that, as they aim to provide insights into staff knowledge and values and also ideas and experiences of children. The index helps in the selection of the activities and whether they are designed for staff, pupils or can be used for both. Many of those designed for staff can be adapted for use with pupils, although some are clearly not suited. One process that helps to facilitate progress through the activities is to invite participants to undertake discussion in groups of three or five. They are working with concepts of majority decision and the idea that to disagree and have a minority viewpoint is legitimate. This not only helps to facilitate decisions, but also models good practice in creating arenas in which there is a voice for all. Nearly all the activities in the book require large sheets of paper and felt-tip pens for groups and whole staff or classes to record decisions, problems or ideas. Most will also require photocopies of materials specified within the activity itself.

Index of Activities

Where Are You in your Handling of Bullying? The Four Types of School

Any teacher wishing to pursue a study of bullying 20 years ago would have found a paucity of literature on the subject, but since the pioneering work of Olweus in Scandinavian, and the subsequent Sheffield Project in the UK, there have been several books and many research papers that inform practice and anti-bullying policies. They have helped schools and colleges to develop and undertake innovative schemes. However, there remain schools and staff within schools who do not know how best to deal with bullying and, even worse, a few who appear not to care.

A recent piece of research (Oliver and Candappa, 2003) funded by the Department for Education and Skills (DfES) concluded that over half of secondary and primary pupils considered bullying to be a problem. High levels of being bullied were reported in many year groups, 28 per cent in Year 8 and 51 per cent in Year 5. Such variation and levels are linked to how bullying is defined, who defines it and what research instrument is used. I will return to these themes later. What was even more significant was that a 'considerable variation was reported in the level of bullying between schools' (Oliver and Candappa, 2003, p. 5). Schools then make a difference and it follows that, within schools, how teachers and other staff work with their pupils, manage their classes and deal with bullying will also make a difference. One of the positive findings of the research was that most pupils expressed positive views about how schools handled incidents. However, there are inconsistencies at individual and school level. There is a small number of adults who say 'it is not my problem' and see it as simply a matter between pupils that they should resolve themselves and that it is a natural part of the social maturation process. Others see it as another issue they have to confront alongside the myriad of topics and innovations which schools are compelled to embrace and act upon. Finally, there are those adults who perceive how pupils feel and what they experience socially and emotionally as an integral part of the learning and the school experience. To them a pupil who is being bullied will be inhibited in their learning and will be failing to derive full academic, social and emotional benefit from being at school.

The attitudes of staff and the culture they nurture will influence which anti-bullying strategies 'best fit' the school, and it is highly likely that anti-bullying practices in themselves help to facilitate change in the school culture. For example, a school that is prepared to look to peer mediation to resolve bullying conveys a clear message that countering bullying is the responsibility of everyone and also that pupils can be trained in skills that mean they are given the power to bring about conflict resolution. It is unlikely to work in a school in which power rests solely with a single person or a small senior management team and the voice of the pupil is neither sought after nor heard, and it is hard to imagine extensive pupil involvement in a school in which the tone is authoritarian and staff themselves feel bullied.

Bullying is a complex subject that arouses high emotions and the language used to describe it demonstrates the range of views held. For some it is a 'scourge' (Pervin and Turner, 1994), others view it as 'The Silent Nightmare' (Smith, 1991). Alternatively, there are those who, whilst they do not sanction it, ask that we should regard it as 'normal' (Maines and

Robinson, 1991). Just as it is regarded differently by individuals, so schools have also responded in different ways. I have noticed that there are basically four stances that schools adopt towards-bullying, although they may also represent stages that they go through as they develop practice.

1 Denial: 'it is not a problem here'.

2 Token: 'we have a policy somewhere'.

3 Moving: 'we have well thought through policy and practice'.

4 Motoring: 'we have clear policy and practices that all know and feel
                 ownership of'.

It would be easy to be swept along a course that leads to Stage 4, but not all schools would see it as either desirable or necessary to bring such radical change to their culture. It may be that this stage needs to be worked towards gradually as part of a programme that invites pupils to have increased responsibility and influence and also perceives their anti-bullying policies to be part of a democratic ethos. A further problem is that of perception, for certain staff might consider the school to be at Stage 1, whilst others feel that the school has a more enlightened approach. Related to notions of inconsistency are the perceptions of parents who also need to know about the school's approach and what ideas and strategies predominate. If they perceive the school to be at a different stage of development or are unaware of how the school addresses bullying, then tensions are inevitable.

ACTIVITY

At what level is the school addressing bullying?

Participants: Staff

Time: 40 minutes

Equipment: List of questions on sheet or transparency, copies of the table **The four stages of school development in dealing with bullying**, large sheets of paper and felt-tip pens.

A facilitator distributes copies of the table amongst staff who consider, in small groups, the following questions and record findings on large sheets of paper.

1 At what stage is this school currently performing?

2 What stage should it aim to achieve?

3 If there is a difference between (2) and (1), what needs to be put in place to achieve (2)?

4 What are the implications of differing views?

Following that, display the sheets, share views and feedback areas of agreement and difference of opinion, and from this devise three key areas which need addressing.

The four stages of school development in dealing with bullying

1 Denial	There is a policy somewhere, written by someone, some time ago;
	bullying is not a problem in this school, but is viewed as a natural part of the growing up process;
	little can or should be done about it;
	if it were to be a concern for us it is important that we keep the issue 'in-house';
	being open about our anti-bullying approach would imply that it is a problem and could be bad publicity for the school.
2 Token	There is a policy, written by a nominated person following a professional development day;
	it is occasionally waved in front of parents and the inspectors;
	few people know what it says, but many rest secure that bullying has been discussed;
	one 'expert' is identified as dealing with the issue and they were the creative force behind the written policy.
3 Moving	The issue is taken seriously and there is a regular review of the policy which incorporates advice and support for pupils, parents and staff;
	staff share effective practice and materials that they have found useful;
	preventative practices are in place;
	ways of dealing with it that are known by adults and pupils in the school.
4 Motoring	The school has clear policy and practices that all know, helped to create and feel ownership of;
	it self-monitors by gathering data about the experience of key players, including parents. All acknowledge that there is bullying beyond the school; nonetheless, staff and pupils combat it in school by constantly adapting, revisiting and experimenting;
	there is recognition of the importance of involving a wider community and of the value of sharing effective practice with parents and other significant parties;
	preventing bullying forms part of a programme that focuses on involving and empowering pupils in playing a positive role in school and making wise choices throughout their lives;
	pupils are supported in developing strategies that not only provide personal protection, but also develop positive peer relationships;
	preventing bullying is synonymous with promoting an ethos in which all pupils who attend the school value and respect each other.

CHAPTER 2

How Do We Know When It Is Bullying?

One of the major problems facing anti-bullying programmes is that of definition – what actually constitutes bullying? This chapter opens with a description of the various forms that bullying can take before moving on to explore the key features of bullying and the language that we associate with it. The activities invite staff and children to examine their own understanding and to create definitions that embrace the understanding of others as well as their own.

Types of Bullying Behaviour

When asked 'what is bullying?' younger children often reply with lists of behaviours such as 'calling people nasty names' and 'hitting someone'. These lists are not definitions in that they are a sentence or two which create boundaries around the term. However, such lists are important in that from them we learn about the experiences of children and we can generate an understanding of the breadth of behaviours that bullying can embrace and become familiar with the ever-changing forms that it can take, especially the advent of 'technobullying' or 'cyberbullying' (bullying through mobile phones and computers). They provide evidence that bullying assumes both *direct* and *indirect* forms, i.e. it is possible to bully without being in the presence of the victim. There are three basic types:

1   *Physical bullying.* Physical bullying is more than punching and kicking and can assume indirect forms, including taking possessions, damaging property or school work with a view to disempower, i.e. there is a physical manifestation of the bullying but no physical pain. Included in such forms of bullying is extortion, where threat of violence leads to the victim giving up money or possessions, and the threat of violence or gestures and body language that is intimidating. Where a disagreement has boiled over into a fight then this is unlikely to be bullying as it lacks the cold intent to disempower. Of course, there will have been intent to hurt and hurt will have been experienced, but it is distinguished from bullying by the equal power status of the fighters.

2 *Verbal bullying.* This is one of the most common forms of bullying as it can have an immediate impact, often in front of an audience, with very little effort on the part of the perpetrator. Name-calling and offensive, threatening and insulting remarks are all forms that this can take and can be directed at or seek to create vulnerable groups. Sexual orientation, ethnic group and learning difficulties are all catalysts for those seeking power at the expense of others. The advent of bullying by mobile phone and computers provides new means by which verbal bullying can be carried out away from the physical presence of the victim.

3 *Social bullying.* This form of bullying incorporates deliberate exclusion from social groups or intimidation within the group. Like other forms it can be direct, with exclusion experienced by the victim, or it can be indirect, that is, carried out away from the victim and not experienced by them until they are informed of it or they attempt to join the group.

It is important to remember that no single form is more hurtful than any other. Social exclusion may cause more pain and disempowerment than physical attack and verbal teasing can leave scars that last a lifetime or certainly beyond those resulting from physical bullying. The impact of bullying is not determined by its form but by the loss of social status, power and the hurt experienced by the victim.

In attempting to help clarify what bullying is, writers have offered models of bullying that seek to differentiate between its various types. For example, Olweus (1993) talks of 'direct' bullying which is carried out face to face and 'indirect' bullying which is more subtle and usually involves a third party, e.g. exclusion or rumour-spreading. Rigby (1996) focuses on the issue of intent in his distinction between 'malign' bullying, which is premeditated and intended, and 'non-malign' which is 'mindless' and considered by the perpetrators to be harmless or just a game. In his discussion of 'non-malign' bullying, he includes a notion of 'educational' bullying in which adults, such as teachers, cause hurt, yet their motive was to do little more than correct errors in work, i.e. there was no intention to cause hurt.

One of the most pernicious and contemporary forms of bullying has many names. Known as 'technobullying', 'cyberbullying' or 'e-bullying', it involves the use of the Internet and e-mail to inflict hurt on others. Apart from psychological pain being inflicted at a distance, what renders it different from other forms of bullying is that the recipient may never have been known personally to the bully and it is, therefore, an indirect form. In this case, unless there is extensive engagement with the bully, the hurt inflicted may also never be known.

Problems with Defining Bullying

A colleague had been working with a pupil who had been experiencing what seemed to be persistent bullying. The pupil was a bright young man but was thought to have a communication disorder. Finding out what had happened to him was a problem for my colleague as the pupil kept repeating the statement 'well, he's not exactly breaking my legs'. After a while my colleague ventured the question 'you keep saying this, but they do not sound like your words. Where do they come from?' The boy looked up and, without emotion, replied 'my tutor'. The message that the pupil appeared to receive was that it had to be an extreme injury before what he was experiencing could be considered as bullying and merited prompt action from the tutor. It did also serve to remind my colleague that encouragement to regard a wide range of behaviours as bullying had clearly avoided at least one teacher. This is not typical of what I find in working with teachers and other professionals who are constantly looking to find effective ways of dealing with bullying and have adopted broad definitions that encapsulate physical, psychological, emotional and social forms of negative action in their understanding of the term 'bullying'.

How bullying is defined impacts upon practice in the way that adults and children make sense of the phenomenon and, therefore, how it might be prevented. However, it is extremely hard to define with accuracy, and many leading writers on the subject have attempted to do so, but with little consistency. What has been achieved is the creation of a vocabulary that helps staff and pupils to formulate their own definition and to distinguish between bullying and other aggressive actions. I do not intend to offer a specific definition here but, instead, I suggest that the process of working towards gleaning pupils' understanding informs the thinking of all parties. Perceptions on the meaning of the term 'bullying' vary but what is important is that they are brought out into the open. For example, as mentioned previously younger pupils, when asked what they understand by 'bullying', often list events that they have either experienced or witnessed, whereas adults usually try to find a sentence or two that embraces their understanding. Definitions constructed by staff occasionally focus on a narrow range of behaviours, usually physical or violent in nature, although others adopt a broader approach that includes intimidation and social exclusion. There are those who would include racially and sexually motivated aggression as bullying and those who would see it as a separate and distinctive form of abuse.

During a recent conference address to teachers I asked delegates to consider a number of scenarios and whether or not specific behaviours fitted in with their definition of bullying. One scenario was, *Danny spits into Billy's drink and forces him to drink it*. After deliberation one delegate stated passionately that she did 'not care whether it was bullying or not, it was unacceptable'. I sympathized with the sentiments but reflected that in the book exhibition attached to the conference were numerous books on 'bullying' and probably hundreds that made mention of it (it also forms part of the title of this book). Dropping the term and replacing it with another equally imprecise term, such as 'unacceptable', may do little more than present another indefinable term. Just as one person's bullying may be another person's 'having a laugh', so there may be different perceptions on what is 'unacceptable' and such differences may inhibit the development of effective policy and practice. However, exploring the meaning of the term 'bullying' through the presentation of 'scenarios' and tables offered later in this chapter will raise awareness and prove helpful in discerning different interpretations and building a vocabulary that represents our personal understanding. Pupils and adults who work in schools need to become aware of the various meanings that 'bullying' can have rather than come to an all-embracing, perfect conclusion.

The *Definitions of bullying from the literature* table (pages 12–13) represents only a small sample of attempts by writers and researchers but illustrates that experts in the field offer a variety of views and yet, in devising policies, schools are encouraged to arrive at their own institutional definition (www.dfes.gov.uk/bullying). Given preordained definitions and working in small groups the activity often proves difficult, serving to illustrate the complexity of defining bullying and that it is difficult to arrive at 'watertight' definitions.

ACTIVITY

Definitions from the literature

Participants: Staff

Time: 40 minutes

Equipment: List of questions on sheet or transparency, copies of **Definitions of bullying from the literature** (p.12–13) and/or **How staff from one school defined bullying** (p.29) large sheets of paper and felt-tip pens.

A facilitator asks individual participants to define bullying and then distributes copies of the chosen table amongst staff who consider questions (1) and (2) in small groups and record their findings on large sheets of paper before returning to the full group and tackling questions (3) and (4).

1 Which definition(s) provide a nearest match to your own thinking (rank order them if it would be helpful)?

2 What are the key concepts that underpin your decision? Write your conclusion on the large piece of paper and share.

3 What are the similarities of, and differences between, the decisions of groups?

4 What are the implications for practice in school?

Definitions of bullying from the literature

Definition	Author	Themes	Rank
A continuum of behaviour which involves the attempt to gain power and dominance over another.	Askew (1989)	1 Concept of a **continuum**; 2 search for **power**.	
Bullying … is … systematic, occurring repeatedly, and it embraces a variety of hurtful actions, including name-calling, social exclusion, having money taken or belongings damaged as well as more obvious physical forms such as hitting and kicking.	Bowers, Smith and Binney (1994)	1 **Repeated** and systematic nature of bullying; 2 **variety of behaviours** that might be included.	
It is deliberately hurtful behaviour: it is repeated often over a period of time; it is difficult for those being bullied to defend themselves.	DfE (1994)	1 **Repetition**; 2 **duration** of action; 3 **the lack of power** of the victim.	
Bullying is a way of being horrible and cruel to another child or group of children. It might happen just once or it can be repeated. The victim may find the behaviour embarrassing, hurtful or humiliating, and be frightened or threatened by it. The bully may not realize this.	Herbert (1996)	1 Against **individuals**; 2 **single or repeated** actions; 3 **hurt/response** of the victim is significant.	

Definitions of bullying from the literature – continued			
Definition	Author	Themes	Rank
Bullying is the wilful, conscious desire to hurt or threaten or frighten someone else. To do this, the bully has to have some sort of power over the victim, a power not always recognizable to the teacher.	Johnstone, Munn and Edwards (1992)	1 **Intent** of bully; 2 **power** over the victim; 3 **teachers may not recognize that power**.	
Bullying is repeated oppression, psychological or physical, of a less powerful person by a more powerful person or group or persons.	Rigby (1996)	1 **Repetition**; 2 **imbalance of power** between bully and victim.	
Bullying is the wilful, conscious desire to hurt another and put him/her under stress. It can be occasional and short-lived, or it can be regular and long-standing.	Tattum (1989)	1 The **intent** behind bullying; 2 it being **a sporadic action** or something more **substantial**.	

What emerges is a picture of different emphasis in the meaning of the term 'bullying' plus a vocabulary that informs understanding bullying. Although they are not the only terms, key concepts covered are usually (similar terms or phrases in brackets):

- *Intent* (deliberate, wilful, conscious, premeditated, predetermined);

- *Hurt* (pain, stress, fright, upset, loneliness) ;

- *Repetition* (more than once, again and again, persistent);

- *Duration* (over a period of time, longstanding);

- *Power* (pressure, strength);

- *Provocation* (called forth, invited).

Looking at Examples

Central to the values promoted in this book is a desire for staff and pupils to engage openly in discussion and debate on the subject of bullying, but this is not always easy. Exploring the meaning of the term 'bullying' with pupils is a sensitive operation because within the groups or classes are pupils that are likely to be involved in it. Direct conversation about experiences may not be productive and can lead to pupils finding it difficult to talk about the issue because it is too personal, threatening or emotive. However, using short scenarios can serve to break down barriers as they permit engagement with ideas and provide a means by which pupils can begin to speak more openly with each other about bullying.

There are many ways that scenarios can be used and I have suggested two activities (pages 14 and 16) which can be viewed as alternatives. They are based upon numerous incidents contained within the *Bullying scenarios: set B* table. Included in the incidents are a number of items that are clearly unlikely to be bullying and are included so that younger pupils, in particular, are not exposed to a long list of negative behaviours. There are also a number of incidents that are similar, sometimes very similar, but it is the slight difference between them that stimulates discussion. When reflecting on the incidents described, adults often relate that they need more information before they can attribute the term 'bullying' to the incident. This may be true, although the pursuit of that information often resembles attempts to 'get to the bottom' of the problem and 'get the whole picture'. However laudable, such pursuits often lead to inconclusive outcomes as to whether an incident is bullying or not as it is often a matter of debate or perception. Hence there is a need to place such emphasis upon working towards a shared understanding and definition. In addition, teachers in primary schools are usually aware of who are involved and what is going on (Lee, 2001) and teachers in secondary schools have a fairly good idea. Although gathering each party's version of what happened and documenting and dating it is good practice, indeed essential, perceiving it to be the 'truth' can be a mistake, for bullying seems to attract a variety of interpretations and a variety of versions of the 'truth'.

ACTIVITY

Working with incidents to construct a definition – set A

Participants: Staff

Time: Version 1: 40 minutes
                Version 2: 70 minutes

Equipment: Photocopies of **Bullying scenarios: set 1** are required and, for Version 1 only, they will need to be cut along the dotted lines.

Version 1: Divide the larger group into six subgroups and ask each one to consider an individual scenario and the related questions for 10–15 minutes. Reconvene the larger group and ask each subgroup to report back on their discussion and responses to questions. Return to the subgroups and, in the light of the broader discussion, create a definition of bullying and consider the implications for policy and practice.

Version 2: Divide the larger group into subgroups and ask each one to consider all the scenarios and the questions for 40–50 minutes. Reconvene the larger group and ask each subgroup to specify which scenario(s) and questions produced the most discussion. Return to the subgroups and, in the light of the broader discussion, consider the implications for policy and practice.

Bullying scenarios: set 1

Intent

Danny spits into Billy's drink and forces him to drink it

Danny spits into a drink and says that he will force Billy to drink it.

1 In selecting Billy is Danny not creating a victim of bullying?
2 If bullying is defined by intent rather than the hurt caused, is there any significant difference between the scenarios?
3 Should intent be given the status that it often has in definitions of bullying?

Hurt

Karl can't read very well but is fine at most other areas of school work. Two girls call him 'thicky' to his face.

Karl can't read very well but is fine at most other areas of school work. Two girls call him 'thicky' behind his back.

Karl can't read very well but is fine at most other areas of school work. Two staff call him 'thicky' behind his back.

1 Should we be working with perpetrators to help them understand the hurt experienced by victims?
2 Should we be working with bystanders to help them understand the hurt experienced by victims?
3 In a preventative approach, should we be working with all pupils and staff to help them understand the hurt experienced by victims?
4 Is it possible to be hurt indirectly by the words of others, even if they are never heard by the person being discussed?

Repetition

Every time Jenny passes Adele she pulls her long hair. She knows that it hurts her.

1 Can a single hurtful action be bullying or does it need to be repeated for it to be bullying?
2 Is there an important distinction to be made between actions that fit into a definition of bullying and relationships that are based upon such actions, i.e. they are repeated?
3 At what stage is intervention desirable?
4 In a preventative approach should there be intervention at the first suspicion of bullying or should we wait until there is confirmation of bullying determined by repetition of the act?

Duration

David gets fed up with Nancy who has been teasing him since they were put into the same class. He lashes out at her with a pencil and cuts her forehead.

1 If bullying lasts over a period of time does it represent a more serious problem for schools and for those charged with dealing with it?
2 Is nasty teasing over a period of time 'bullying'?
3 Has the term 'bullying' been associated more with physical acts than name-calling and social exclusion?
4 If both are bullies then where does the power rest in this relationship?

▶

Bullying scenarios: set 1 – continued

Power

Andrew tells George that, if he does not give him his dinner money every Monday, then he will beat him up.

1 Does the above represent the kind of action that leads to one person having power over another or are there other, more subtle, actions?
2 Does the 'asymmetry of power' become established after an initial exploratory act, or do pupils know instinctively who are the powerful and who are powerless?
3 What are the implications for preventative strategies in schools?
4 How much should an anti-bullying policy apply to adults in a school?
5 Does the status and power of the perpetrator matter as much as the bullying behaviour?

Provocation

John likes to gain the attention of his peers. Occasionally he does so by calling them names until they respond aggressively. He then tells the staff that he has been bullied.

1 In the case of those who provoke or invite bullying, who possesses the power that is central to our understanding of bullying?
2 Given that the name 'bully' is often given to the person who has power over another, is John a 'provocative victim'?
3 Are perpetrators without responsibility if they respond to the 'provocative victim'?
4 It is one of the least used terms in definitions of bullying, is the term 'provocation' useful in informing our understanding?

ACTIVITY

Working with incidents to construct a definition – set B

Participants: Staff and pupils

Time :   Version 1: 50 minutes
                Version 2: 60 minutes

Equipment: Photocopies of **Bullying scenarios: set 2** are required for Version 1 and laminated cards will need to be prepared for Version 2.

Version 1: Distribute photocopies of scenarios and request that small groups consider each scenario and decide whether they are:

(a) definitely bullying (label as D);
(b) might be bullying   (label as M);
(c) not bullying   (label as N).

Reconvene the larger group or class and compare decisions. For both version 1 and version 2 it is worth considering what additional information would need to have been present in the 'might be' incidents for them to be placed in the 'definitely bullying' pile.

Version 2: Another method is to make larger laminated card copies of 'definitely bullying', 'might be bullying' and 'not bullying', and smaller laminated strips of each incident. Initially each incident is considered in small groups and, having discussed and debated them, place them on the appropriate large laminated card. In the case of younger pupils it may be preferable to have larger cards or perhaps illustrations, fewer incidents and boxes into which each card can be placed. (If you position the three large cards so that there is a small space between them you will notice that staff will place some smaller scenario cards over that space thereby bridging the gap — they are the definitely/maybe bullying incidents! Children are rarely that uncertain).

In the debriefing, it is important to consider how decisions were reached in groups, such as:

(a) Was a majority decision system employed?
(b) Did anyone feel excluded or their views not valued?
(c) What are the implications for differences in opinion in a school that seeks to prevent bullying?

Bullying scenarios: set 2

Karl cannot read very well but is okay at most other things in school. Two girls in the class call him 'thicky' but only behind his back.

Jane puts a worm in Julie's bag. She knows that Julie is frightened of worms.

Mick tells Chris that, if he doesn't do everything that he says, he will tell the teacher that Chris was being naughty.

Karl cannot read very well but is okay at most other things in school. Two girls in the class call him 'thicky' to his face.

Jennifer has a hearing impairment and some of the pupils in the class deliberately whisper so that she cannot hear them talking.

Tariq has asthma and cannot do games every week. One of the girls is always mentioning this and making him feel bad about it.

David tells George that if he does not give him his dinner money he is going to beat him up.

Amanda and Sally refuse to speak to Jane for a whole week.

Philip's parents have divorced and Mark tells everyone in the class.

Keith and Alan refuse to let Asmat play with them.

Keith and Alan refuse to let Richard play with them.

David kicks Sally's bag and it goes all over the classroom.

Harry kicks Mike's bag on purpose and it goes all over the playground.

James always nudges Max when he passes him in the playground.

Every time Jenny goes past Adele in the playground she pulls her long hair and she knows that it hurts.

Sarah and her family go to church on Sundays. Two boys in her class at school call her names because of this.

Bullying scenarios: set 2 – continued

Ben spends all the playtime following Ash and tapping his arm, even though Ash says that he wants to be left alone.

Caroline's father has just been made unemployed. Helen tells all the class and starts to call her 'little poor girl'.

Natalie has nicknamed Pauline 'scruffy'.

Mick, Jake and Paul refuse to speak to Harry for a whole week.

Danny spits into Billy's drink and forces him drink it.

Danny spits into a drink and says that he will force Billy to drink it.

Natalie has nicknamed Pauline 'scruffy' and, as a result, all the class are beginning to call her that too.

Helen keeps telling other children that Mandy smells – it is true.

Helen keeps telling other children that Mandy smells.

Karl cannot read very well but is okay at most other things in school. Two staff in the school call him 'thicky' but only behind his back.

David is fed up with the teasing that Nancy does in class, at his expense, and he lashes out at her with a pencil and scratches her forehead.

David is fed up with the teasing that Nancy does in class and he lashes out at her with a pencil and scratches her forehead.

Amanda and Sally refuse to speak to Jane for a whole week because she has been telling the teacher that they bring sweets to school, which is against the rules.

Amanda and Sally refuse to speak to Jane for a whole week because she has been whispering about them to some boys in the class.

For no obvious reason, Amanda and Sally refuse to speak to Jane for a whole week.

Every time that Zechan walks into the class a group of pupils laugh and whisper to each other.

A group of older boys will not let anyone else play football at break.

The youngest boy in the class is helped by two of the oldest ones.

In the corner of the room Fahana is working with John and they are giggling about something.

Teresa and Sally talk with Jenny during the lunchtime and they talk about what they watched on television.

Nicholas and Ben play football with Adam who is often left out at playtimes.

Emma and Charlie help Darren with his reading in class.

When Karl leaves his bag in the classroom, two boys from the class sneak in and pour water into it.

John likes to gain the attention of his peers. Occasionally he does so by calling them names until they respond aggressively. He then tells the staff that he has been bullied.

When Jane is not looking one of her classmates writes all over her neat piece of work and spoils it.

The following are examples of the issues raised by pupils of all ages when discussing them. Staff using the scenarios to raise awareness will find it helpful to be aware of matters that usually arise and the following will help them to consider questions and responses on them.

Jane puts a worm in Julie's bag. She knows that Julie is frightened of worms.

This is often seen as bullying because the worm is seen as an unpleasant creature and there has been deliberate exploitation of a fear.

Caroline's father has just been made unemployed. Helen tells all the class and starts to call her 'little poor girl'.

Drawing attention to a parent being made unemployed arouses as much indignation as the subsequent name-calling. Throughout the activity the context and motive behind the act will prove as meaningful as the act itself.

Mick tells Chris that, if he doesn't do everything that he says, he will tell the teacher that Chris was being naughty.

Pupils comment on the familiarity of this form of behaviour and that they have experienced similar threats.

Philip's parents have split up and Mark tells everyone in the class.

The motive behind Mark informing everyone in the class is vital; after all he might have been trying to be helpful or even acting under instructions from Philip. This can lead into a useful discussion on the nature of 'intent'.

Natalie has nicknamed Pauline 'scruffy' and now all the pupils are beginning to call her that too.

The choice of this as bullying is based upon interpretation of intent and resultant hurt. Children comment that calling Pauline 'scruffy' would be bullying if she was concerned by it and it 'depends whether she likes being called scruffy'.

David is fed up with the teasing that Nancy does in class, at his expense, and he lashes out at her with a pencil and scratches her forehead.

Little is made of the difference in the two scenarios, i.e. the fact that David is bullied in the first but we are not sure in the second. However, much is made of who is the perpetrator and if Nancy's actions merited the label 'bully' or David's contribution is little more than retaliation. Pupils emphasize that he was 'getting back' not bullying and 'it served her right', 'revenge was not bullying', 'Nancy is definitely the bully'. Occasionally they state that 'they are as bad as one another'.

Keith and Alan refuse to let Asmat play with them. Keith and Alan refuse to let Richard play with them.

The problem of distinguishing between racism and bullying is evident here. The apparent racial overtone of the exclusion of Asmat usually arouses more outrage than the experience of Richard, although, on occasions, astute pupils observe that Richard may also not be white or that Asmat is a UK citizen unlike Richard. In general, an act is more likely to be defined as bullying when pupils are in sympathy with thevictim. Conversely there is less outrage if others understand why they are being bullied.

Throughout this activity the furore with which many incidents are greeted demonstrates the passion that the children feel about bullying and contrasts with the thoughtful, more considered manner in which staff formulate definitions and reflect upon the subject. From the analysis of working with many groups of children of a variety of ages it would appear that pupils define bullying:

- by outcome; that is the hurt caused, rather than the act itself;

- by the more outrageous or repulsive the act and the emotions it aroused;

- with 'hurt' and 'intent' as predominant strands;

- by how much children can relate to or sympathize with the experience of the victims.

There is less concern for acts that are repeated, take place over a period of time or are a manifestation of power of one pupil over another. Younger children have a broad definition of bullying based upon individual, hurtful acts that were intended, whereas adults often view bullying as a phenomenon that only becomes serious if the hurt is repeated and a relationship predicated on bullying becomes established. The difference in these stances may lead to staff not appearing to take reported bullying as seriously as their pupils, and underlines the merits of sharing views on what may or may not be bullying.

The Vocabulary of Bullying

Staff leading sessions aimed at raising awareness on the vocabulary and definitions of bullying will find it useful to become familiar with the issues that arise from the vocabulary and the discussion cited here which is from the literature on, and research into, bullying.

Intent: Did the Perpetrator Mean It?

Intent focuses on motives, what was meant to happen. Perpetrators often offer the defence that they did not intend to cause hurt and, in some cases, this may be true. When reflecting on their actions, pupils sometimes state that their intention was not to hurt, but simply to gain admiration or social prestige from their actions. They may also invoke the idea that they were 'only teasing' and this has led to the use of 'nasty teasing' in certain definitions (Ahmad, Whitney and Smith, 1991). In the table *How staff from one school defined bullying* (page 29) Mrs P refers to 'unconscious' bullying, where the action felt like bullying to the victim yet a notion of considered intent was not present. In many respects, this mirrored Rigby's idea of a 'non-malign' concept in which not all forms of bullying are a consequence of deliberate intent to hurt, but which could be construed by others as bullying. The significance of intent to any act of bullying cannot be overstated, neither can its influence on how it is dealt with by adults. What perpetrators of bullying declare they intend to do can be disempowering, whether or not the declaration is acted out in any form, because in saying they will do something to someone they create a vulnerable pupil, a victim.

> *Danny spits into Billy's drink and forces him to drink it.*

> *Danny spits into a drink and says that he will force Billy to drink it.*

Whether it is pupils or adults who are examining scenarios the above two incidents nearly always cause outrage, usually based on the repulsion that the act of spitting generates. However, it is when the two are examined together that discussion focuses on the idea that the intent need not be linked to hurting Billy directly, but upon demeaning him in his absence. The first incident is usually seen as definitely bullying but, in the second, the fact that we are unaware whether or not he gets to drink from the tainted can causes doubt and debate. In both cases the intent is clear.

Hurt: Did It Cause Physical, Psychological or Emotional Pain?

The responsibility for identifying actions as hurtful often falls on victims. Intent to hurt may have been in the minds of bullies, but confirmation of bullying would only be by evidence from their victims that their action generated fear, distress or pain. The hurt experienced by a child who is being bullied is not to be underestimated and, in considering definitions, pupils sometimes look closely at the action itself – what happened? – when more consideration might be given to its impact – what was the effect? Bullied pupils are able to report hurt experienced, yet so often they find it difficult to say anything about their experiences in case any intervention leads to increased stress, social isolation or loss of already low self-esteem. Creating cultures in which to tell is seen as acceptable means providing sources that will listen, although it may be the case that the initial revelation comes at home and to someone in the family. Given that hurt revealed comes to the school from another source, it is important to establish accessible arenas and sympathetic staff.

> *Karl can't read very well but is fine at most other areas of school work. Two girls call him 'thicky' to his face.*

> *Karl can't read very well but is fine at most other areas of school work. Two girls call him 'thicky' behind his back.*

> *Karl can't read very well but is fine at most other areas of schoolwork. Two staff call him 'thicky' behind his back.*

At first glance there appears to be little difference between the above incidents yet what separates these scenarios generates extensive discussion amongst staff and pupils. The first statement is usually assigned to the 'definitely bullying' category with expressions of outrage, although both staff and children usually add that they have heard worse terms. The second generates doubts, especially amongst pupils, who relate that they occasionally make negative comments about their peers but would not like this to be seen as bullying. It is when the third scenario is reflected upon that sensitive issues begin to be developed. Staff often state that they have heard this kind of term when 'steam is being let off' in the staffroom but pupils, especially younger ones, are often shocked and identify this as bullying. It is the status and power of the name-caller that leads to reflective discussion and, being the only incident where adults are amongst the perpetrators, it raises the issue of their role in perpetuating and promoting bullying. Again the subject of whether bullying demands that someone experiences hurt directly before the term 'bullying' is employed comes to the fore.

Repetition: Was the Act Repeated Time after Time?

How often incidents happen can be a factor in measuring seriousness, indeed whether it constitutes bullying at all. Byrne (1994) suggests that bullying 'lasts for weeks, months, even years. Therefore it does not include isolated incidents' and Olweus (1993) uses 'repeatedly and over time' to exclude less serious events, although he goes on to acknowledge that a single serious instance of harassment could be regarded as bullying. Seriousness, a *qualitative* notion, is the basis of the judgements being made here, but it is set in an argument about the more *quantitative* concept of repetition.

Every time Jenny passes Adele she pulls her long hair. She knows that it hurts her.

As mentioned before, when asked for their understanding of the word 'bullying', pupils often, quite naturally, respond by listing behaviours rather than seeking to formulate an all-embracing sentence or two that encapsulates their meaning. They use words or phrases such as 'picked on', 'on purpose', 'nasty' and 'meant to' to embellish their lists. Rarely do they use ideas of repetition, although it features in adult definitions (pages 12, 13 and 29) and staff in schools use the concept of repetition as one of the measures that determine the seriousness of what is happening. If bullying is first and foremost defined by concepts of intent and hurt, then there is a dilemma here. The first occasion that Jenny pulled Adele's hair may be seen as exploratory, a way of assessing whether it hurts, but alternatively, she is likely to have known that she was about to inflict pain and that she made the deliberate choice of Adele as someone who merited attention.

Duration: How Long Has It Been Going On?

Duration and repetition appear closely linked since, for an incident to be repeated, a period of time must have elapsed and they imply something more long standing. Few have gone as far as Lowenstein (1978) who imposed a six-month period on the duration of events before the application of the term 'bullying'. In contrast La Fontaine's (1991) analysis of telephone calls from a 'bullying hotline' revealed that the hurt felt by victims of bullying need not have resulted from actions that took place over a period of time.

David gets fed up with Nancy who has been teasing him since they were put into the same class. He lashes out at her with a pencil and cuts her forehead.

I was undertaking research in a primary school when this incident occurred. Nancy was always making fun of her peers, usually through hurtful comments and David was included in her chosen group of the 'picked on'. Few who spent any time in the class could not fail to be aware of what she was doing and the teacher had attempted to stop the name-calling and her belittling of others, but it seemed to make little difference. When David reacted so violently, the teacher, in the heat of the moment, diffused the situation by telling him to leave the room and labelled his behaviour 'bullying'.

This scenario leads to considerable discussion amongst both staff and pupils, and invariably focuses less on the behaviours of the two pupils involved and more on the attribution of the label 'bully'. Discussion also centres on whether the period of time that Nancy has called David names means that her actions are more serious than David's reactions and whether reactions qualify as bullying. One often arrived at conclusion is that they are both bullies and, consequently, victims!

Power: Why Do Children Need to Bully?

Power is central to bullying. Olweus (1991) states that bullying is indicative of an 'asymmetric power imbalance' with bullies being stronger, physically and/or psychologically than their victims. Greater power may be a matter of perception and only seen as such by the victims, but that is sufficient to upset the equality in power in the relationship. Physical size and strength are not the only factors that can cause an imbalance of power, and less obvious factors such as a family background can influence the equilibrium of a relationship. The most prolific bully that I have encountered was short and slight in stature and from a family background that gave no indication that bullying was central to the family dynamics, but he had a presence that terrified his peers in both primary and secondary school.

> Andrew tells George that, if he does not give him his dinner money every Monday, then he will beat him up.

Whenever asked to list the scenarios in order of their seriousness, pupils place the threatening behaviour of Andrew near to, if not at, the top. It is not just the promised violence that leads to this endorsement but the apparent power that he possesses over George. They often comment that he does not have to 'beat him up', for the threat alone is sufficient to make George part with his money. Discussion with both the professionals and their pupils has enhanced my view that there are two forms of 'asymmetric power'. First, there are those who establish their power over others *by action* through direct contact or communication. They have 'relationships' with certain pupils that render those pupils powerless to respond to the aggressive attention of the perpetrator. Second, there are those who acquire their power over their peers without having to take any direct forms of action. Their power is based upon *the status* within the social network of the class or school and their presence alone is sufficient to disempower others in the classroom or school.

Provocation: Did the Victim Invite the Attention of the Bully?

Provocation is the term used least by writers and researchers, perhaps because it is taken for granted that victims would not invite or welcome being bullied. However, the identification of a small subgroup of victims of bullying who provoke and gain gratification from the aggressive attention of others, the 'provocative victims' (Stephenson and Smith, 1987) presents a problem for those who seek to find an all-embracing definition. Their existence also raises questions about responsibility for actions and allocation of blame, although whether the victim was acting provocatively or not may be of little significance as a decision to respond rests with the bully, provoked or otherwise.

> John likes to gain the attention of his peers. Occasionally he does so by calling them names until they respond aggressively. He then tells the staff that he has been bullied.

Here is an example of the 'provocative victim', the initiator of negative behaviour who demands the harmful attention of peers in order to ensure the attention of staff, the blame of others or both. I have worked with a pupil who would throw himself to the ground when no other pupils were near him and then reported a violent assault to a member of staff, but he refused to name the pupils for fear of retribution. His motivation was the attention of those in power and he managed to achieve it. There was no provocation of others. He, like the 'provocative victim', calls into question the notion of the victim as always being powerless and they can be highly manipulative and single minded in pursuing their own needs.

An Internet site regarding bullying offers advice to parents that 'if your child says he/she is being bullied then he/she is being bullied' (www.bullying.co.uk). Although all reported events should be taken seriously, there are dangers in this advice. It implies that the sole arbiter of whether bullying has taken place is the apparent victim, that no provocation was present and it provides opportunities for false accusations, erroneous deployment of negative labels and miscarriages of some form of justice.

Questionnaires with Children

When working with younger children illustrations of scenes that include potential bullying incidents lead to exploration of their views. One less sophisticated, but less time-consuming, method of exploring pupils understanding from about the age of eight years upwards is a simple questionnaire which will be considered in Chapter 5. Amongst their many uses, questionnaires provide an opportunity to explore the difference, if any, between bullying and hurtful or unpleasant teasing. Teasing can be both malicious and playful, whereas bullying can only appear to be the former. In research I sometimes use the phrase 'nasty teasing' which has been deployed to distinguish the forms of teasing (Smith, 1991).

My own research results have confirmed the significance of 'hurt' and responses from children generated a feeling of an imbalance of power, but they rarely included other terms. 'Hurt' manifests itself in various forms. There is 'hurt' that is a consequence of an action that damages feelings – 'it is when you hurt inside – it is something to make people upset and hurt their feelings' – or hurt that results in physical, emotional or social nature pain that is linked to the reaction of the recipient – 'where someone pushes you and hurts you inside by calling you names or doing things you don't like'. Other forms include premeditation – 'I think bullying is when someone is out to hurt you and is determined to do it in the most hurtful way' – ideas of power – 'forcing someone to do something' – and demonstrations of outrage – 'it is a desire to hurt someone and it is nasty'. Even such a seemingly simple idea of the hurt that bullying can cause assumes a variety of meanings for pupils. There was a solitary recognition of 'repetition' – 'something that someone keeps doing every day to you'. This pupil continued with that nasty teasing was not as serious as bullying, which may have been related to a subsequent admission of having teased 'for a bit of a laugh'. He was not the only pupil to perceive teasing as potentially enjoyable, illustrating the value of pupils sharing their understanding and discussing how impact and perception of events can be different.

Talking with Bullies and Victims

It is helpful to examine any definition that is contained within your school policy using the six components listed above (pages 20–24) and to see whether it fulfils all of them. They also help to provide a structure for questions to those involved that avoid the search for what happened after bullying has been reported. Before looking at the how the language of bullying can inform conversations with those involved *it is essential to emphasize here that all staff who become aware that bullying could be occurring, should write down what they see and what is said by all parties, ensure that it is dated and ensure actions taken are also noted. Logging information is an essential aid when complex cases of bullying emerge, especially those involving parents. Such records should be kept and not deleted or thrown out.*

One of the most common consequences of discovering bullying is the questioning by adults of the key parties, i.e. the victims and the bully or bullies. This is often undertaken with two questions in mind:

- What happened?

- Who is to blame?

The first is an attempt to glean as much factual information as possible and search for 'the truth'. However, the problem with this is that, as mentioned before, there are likely to be various versions of 'the truth' and few facts emerge, just various 'truths'. It is not in the interest of perpetrators to say what happened and admit responsibility because they believe, sometimes rightly, that the adult's prime motive is to find someone to punish. In the case of the victim, despite encouragement to tell on bullies, they fear the power of bully or the subsequent social isolation that follows revealing what happened.

Regarding the second question, who initiated the bullying is difficult to ascertain as a chance remark or an accident can lead to the development of an incident. Again who started it seems inexorably connected to the task of finding someone to punish, rather that resolving the relationship problem.

Based on the vocabulary of bullying questions have been suggested by teachers and teaching assistants with whom I have worked and are listed in *Questions linked to the language of bullying* (see below). They are no more than a starting point for gathering information, not the best way nor the only way, just the beginning of a discussion. These questions are linked to a desire to gather information and avoid accusing or blaming, but it is essential to avoid labelling anyone as a bully or victim.

Questions linked to the language of bullying			
Key term	Main question(s)	Specific question: possible bully (B)	Specific question: possible victim (V)
Intent	Was there a clear intention of the bully or bullies to hurt?	What did you mean to happen? Did you mean to cause hurt?	Did he/she mean this to happen?
Hurt	Did the victim of the bullying feel hurt by the bully or bullies and was the perpetrator aware of hurt?	Did you know whether you hurt V or not?	Has this hurt you? How has this hurt you? Does B know that you are hurt?
Repetition	Was it more than a one-off act?	Has this happened more than once? How often has this happened?	Has this happened more than once? How often has this happened?

▶

Questions linked to the language of bullying – continued			
Key term	Main question(s)	Specific question: possible bully (B)	Specific question: possible victim (V)
Duration	Have the events been taking place over a period of time?	How long have you been behaving this way towards V? How long has this kind of thing being going on?	How long has this kind of thing being going on?
Power	Was there an imbalance in power or feeling of powerlessness?	How do you feel when you are in V's company?	How do you feel when you are in B's company?
Provocation	Did the victim play any part in gaining the attention of the bullies?	Did V do anything to make you notice him/her?	Did you do anything to make B notice you?

A Model of Bullying: Moving from a Bullying Action to a Bullying Relationship

Breaking bullying down into its component parts, highlighting the discussion within each of those selected parts and raising relevant questions, indicates the complexity of the challenge of finding consensus on definitions of bullying. The activities that have been suggested here shed light on that complexity and it is important to recognize that the journey may be of more significance than the destination. Having stated that it is likely that any policy on bullying will offer a definition that might be accompanied by a phrase 'and there may be other actions that are considered to be bullying, but which do not fit exactly into our given definition'.

One way that I have found to be successful in working both with adults and pupils is to use a diagram which uses the component parts of bullying and which seeks to distinguish between a single event that might be bullying and something more long term. Bullying can be about what pupils do to each other occasionally and, usually more seriously, it can be the centre or basis of a relationship. It is my view that the modern usage of the term 'bullying' embraces two key notions at opposite ends of a continuum and that most bullying and teasing occurs along that continuum.

At one end is a *bullying action* where bullying takes place only occasionally and may not always have a lasting impact upon the relationship or does not provide the sole basis for that relationship, yet hurt was experienced and was meant to be experienced. One basic way to distinguish between bullying and accidental hurt is the intent of the perpetrator and, therefore, this and the hurt caused provide the key elements of a bullying action. The development of a power imbalance begins here and to ignore such behaviours could mean that they are repeated, take place over a period of time, the imbalance becomes institutionalized and a *bullying relation-*

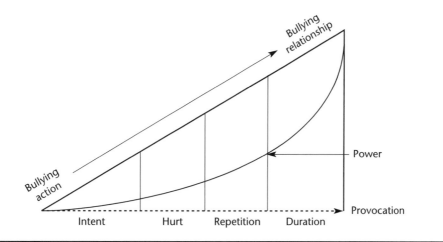

Figure 2.1 From bullying action to bullying relationship

ship becomes established. If bullying actions continue they become central to the relationship, indeed appear to determine it. Throughout it is important to take into consideration whether genuine provocation is present and not the 'she started it' style of excuse that perpetrators can invoke. This continuum is not a definition of bullying in itself, but is offered as a practical model designed to help staff and pupils work towards conceptualizing bullying in the context of their schools. The idea of the continuum also serves to assist in the development of a vocabulary to support children in distinguishing between bullying and other behaviours. I have used it with adults and children in schools, and noted that both parties find this model informs discussion and debate and offers an easily remembered visual summary that incorporates essential terminology.

Teachers and the Definition Task

An anti-bullying policy usually opens with a definition to focus readers, and it would be easy to assume consensus and that there is agreement amongst staff about what bullying is. Let us consider the views of teachers from one primary school, set in a medium-sized town, with approximately 250 pupils and serving a mixed catchment area. In interviews I asked them for their definitions of bullying; although they already had one in their policy document, no one used it or knew it. They were a thoughtful and reflective group, and acknowledged that defining bullying was a difficult task for them. One teacher, Mrs R, felt that shared understanding of terminology might form a key component in generating policy and practice.

> *When you work in a school ... if different teachers are holding different definitions in their head, then ... we have almost lost before we start, because we are not thinking along the same lines. I don't see how we can come to any policy decisions or actually help the child.*

Her view was exactly what I found amongst the staff, for they held disparate definitions which may have been because of the lack of attention given to the issue in the school. The teachers drew upon the same vocabulary, such as 'intent' and 'repetition', to place boundaries around their understanding as shown in *How staff from one school defined bullying*. The headteacher, Mr B's, reaction was linked to his role, despite mentioning premeditation, he resorted to the potential impact upon him as the headteacher, rather than seeking to find a form of words that encapsulated his view. His appraisal of the situation in the school seemed to be a reflection on the dilemma that any headteacher faces admitting to a bullying problem in times when schools are competing for pupils and concerned about their public image.

Adults, like children, construct bullying in a variety of ways. They rarely list behaviours in the way that children often do, but there are distinguishing features in staff versions. The table of staff definitions (page 29) illustrates these and includes:

- seeing bullying as a continuum with verbal interactions at one end and more physical behaviours at the other;

- a range of aggressive behaviours that moves through from teasing to continual abuse along which bullying fits;

- listing forms incorporating 'teasing', 'bullying', 'verbal' and 'physical' elements;

- statements, usually two or three sentences, that embrace their meaning;

- a mixture of the above.

It would be easy to see the differences amongst staff as problematic, but in addressing dissimilarity they began to consider practical implications and made tensions explicit. It proved to be the beginning of a journey that moved the school from the assumption that there was shared understanding to disclosing ideas and contradictions, and enhancing practice.

When asked to define 'bullying' staff in schools often relate that they are doing so for the first time. There is also a certain circumspection that may be attributed to the emotional distance from a bullying event that adults are able to adopt. Unlike parents and children, who may be more directly involved, adults in schools are able to maintain a distance, perhaps aimed at ensuring impartiality. When working with education professionals the inability to arrive at a precise form of words does not seem like indecisiveness, but more an acknowledgement that precision is problematic, even undesirable. Herein lies a dilemma for, while it is important to recognize that a *need for precision* should be juxtaposed with a *need for flexibility* and openness of interpretation, the pressure to manage bullying in schools demands clarity of thinking and shared understanding.

The term 'bullying' has become more liberally used which means that there may be pressure on schools to develop a common understanding between all parties. Anti-bullying policies that begin with a definition have the advantage of focusing thoughts, but they also have disadvantages. For example, an imposed definition can be remote from pupils and amount to a powerful group imposing their comprehension of the term on others, yet I believe that any discussion of the term 'bullying' should include those closest to it, the pupils. Talking to adults and children, it is obvious that they are often exploring the meaning of 'bullying' for the first time with resultant self-doubt, questioning and contradiction. In a school culture in which children are encouraged 'to tell' and seek support of adults it seems crucial that all parties have a vocabulary that helps awareness of what is being reported. It may be that bullying *cannot* be defined exactly; indeed the evidence here would suggest that this is the case. However, with such an emotive term being employed extensively in contemporary education, the process of seeking meaning

How staff from one school defined bullying		
Person	Definition	Themes
Mrs L:	There is a sense of deliberate hurt behind it … . I think I'm inclined to believe that hurt wasn't the prime intention, the response is the prime intention.	Hurt, Intent
Mrs M:	I consider it could be a one-off event but more often than not I would think it's persistent. I think of it as persistent abuse rather than a one-off thing, but now I've come to realize that it can be a one-off incident.	Repetition, Duration
Mrs A:	I would define bullying as something that's consistent, something that happens on a regular basis The piggy in the middle is actually distressed.	Hurt, Repetition, Duration
Mrs C:	Bullying is something that maybe works on a continuum, if it's happening all the time and it's upsetting the child.	Hurt, Repetition, Duration
Mrs P:	Anybody who uses their strength, their size or their intellect to put down or upset or hurt anybody else to me is a form of bully … it's mostly deliberate, but sometimes unconscious.	Power, Hurt, Intent(?)
Mrs F:	Bullying … intimidates someone else, or makes another person feel uncomfortable or diminishes the other person's efforts.	Hurt
Mrs S:	It's where somebody is putting pressure on another in a way that is hurtful to them.	Power, Hurt
Mr :Y	I think that it is a whole range of behaviours, ranging from teasing, to minor non-verbal physical incidents, right up to systematic physical abuse of another person.	Hurt
Ms J:	Somebody is being victimized … makes them feel like somebody is imposing themselves.	Power
Mr B:	Physical violence of the type that threatens to hospitalize a kid. That's what causes me the problems. It is not just a flare-up but is usually predetermined and usually the same children … but you've got to grade it. I recognize that name-calling is hurtful and damaging to a person's confidence.	Intent, Hurt
Mr H:	Where an individual or individuals experience verbal or physical abuse repeatedly — I would have thought.	Repetition, Hurt
Mrs R:	It's something persistent. The other thing that I'd thought about is that it's something that happens for this person more than once and there is some form of premeditation. It also involves more than one person … you need a bully, somebody who is going to in some way persecute the victim … another person is hurt in some way by the act being done by the aggressor, the bully.	Intent, Hurt, Repetition, Duration, Power
Mrs L:	I think bullying is something that maybe works on a continuum, if it's happening all the time and it's upsetting the child, then I would call it bullying.	Duration, Hurt

has the potential to benefit all groups. Engaging in reflection on terminology has benefits of rendering the issue an open one, developing a common vocabulary and highlighting that there are various perceptions of what is meant by 'bullying'. The process that explores differences in meaning and shared viewpoints may be of more value to the school than any final product that embodies the standpoints of a variety of parties, and it helps schools to move away from ever-refined definitions of bullying to clearer thinking and practice.

CHAPTER 3

Who Are Involved in Bullying?

This chapter looks at the various groups involved in bullying and concludes that it involves more than just the bully and the victim. Through case studies, research evidence and story a diverse model of the involved emerges, with emphasis placed upon the role of bystanders as well as how schools can support parents whose children are mixed up in bullying.

A simplistic definition of a 'victim' might be one who is bullied, and a 'bully' would be the perpetrator of such acts, but if defining bullying is complex and problematic then this translates into problems in applying such labels to the involved. Acceptance of a definition based solely on notions of intent and hurt would mean that a single aggressive act could lead to deployment of such pejorative labels as 'bully'. If use of the term 'bullying' is increasing, embracing a wide variety of forms of negative action, then it follows that there will be an equally extensive use of the terms 'bully' and 'victim'. Any policy, or practices, that label pupils 'bully' and 'victim' runs the risk that these terms can have a negative impact on pupils' self-esteem and potentially on parents with whom schools may well need to work co-operatively. 'Bully' and 'victims' are the terms used in the literature, and this book is no exception, but, especially in the case of the victim, use of them is likely to compound the damage done. They are emotive terms and can 'fan the flames' of conflict rather than facilitate resolution, and they also represent a model of bullying that confines it to immediate participants, allowing others to avoid both influence and responsibility and seeing themselves as not involved. As with much of the literature on bullying many of the ways of countering bullying focus on the immediate participants – the 'bully' and their 'victim' – and, while what follows aims to develop understanding of these key players, there is also a discussion of the further group of key players, the rest of us – the wrongly named 'non-involved'.

Victims

'It is one thing to observe patterns of social behaviour. It is another to experience them'

(Cullingford and Brown, 1995).

ACTIVITY

Who are the victims?

Participants: Staff

Time: 30 minutes

Equipment: Pen and paper.

Consider the pupils (class, tutor group or group) that you are currently working with or have taught recently.

1 Who were being 'picked on' or bullied?

2 How did you know?

3 What factors do you think led them being selected for bullying?

Share your views with a colleague and write a list of the characteristics or reasons that you have identified as leading to those particular pupils being bullied.

Why do some pupils become victims? There are many answers to this question. For example, a pupil may possess an attribute that attracts the attention of bullies such as:

- problems with learning;

- no problems with learning, indeed seen as a 'swot';

- physical attributes/difficulties;

- a lack of appropriate social skills or capacity to make friends;

- behaviour problems;

- a mixture of the above.

Victims are, in one way or another, often different from the social norm and that difference is evident and known by others. The significance of a pupil being different as a determinant of being bullied has been mentioned in research into pupil perceptions of victims of bullying. Cullingford and Brown (1995) found that 36 per cent of pupils felt that pupils were victims because they were different and that difference could be something as minor as hair colour. Once singled out, victims run the risk of becoming generally unpopular, socially rejected, a 'common enemy' and bullied by more than the initiator.

Another reason why particular children are bullied is connected to theories of attachment. Developed from research with pre-school age children, Cowie, Boulton and Smith (1992) link children with 'ambivalent-avoidant' attachment relationships with their parents, i.e.

they receive inconsistent and haphazard levels of care and doubt their own ability to influence the caregiver, to an increased likelihood of being bullied. If this were the case then identifying such children as vulnerable would be difficult, although it may manifest itself in evidence of the child having a low sense of self-worth.

Low self-esteem, whether a cause or consequence of bullying, distances some pupils from their peers. Pupils with low self-esteem are more likely to be bullied than their peers with higher self-esteem, although it seems doubtful that low self-esteem, in itself, encourages other pupils to target an individual initially and it is more likely to be the way that the bullied pupil responds which leads to incidents (Sharp, 1995). Amongst the implications of this is recognition that it may well be too late to leave intervention until a bullying action has turned into a bullying relationship. The damage will already have been done and the pupil has been identified by peers as powerless, low in self-esteem and incapable of mustering an effective defence. They are then in need of support from others, be they adults or their peers. Simply urging such pupils 'to tell' implies that they possess the courage and power to do so, and to take the consequences that might result. Adults in classrooms often know who is involved or vulnerable (it was probably not difficult to identify them in the activity *Who are the victims?* – page 32) and supporting them when they come forward with information would be part of effective, but difficult, practice in countering bullying. The major dilemma faced in working with victims is whether there should be a requirement for them to change their behaviour or appearance in order that they do not draw the attention of bullies or whether they have the right to continue to look and act in any way that they wish.

ACTIVITY

Who should change their behaviour?

Participants: Staff

Time: 20–30 minutes

Equipment: Pen and paper.

In small groups, consider whether pupils who are being bullied should be required to change their behaviour or appearance or whatever is attracting the attention of the bully. Make a list of situations that might demand change and consider how best this might be achieved. Follow this with a full group discussion that considers the implications for the anti-bullying policy.

In my own research, pupils have identified reasons why children say that others in their class are being bullied. Although they were not asked to name anyone, they clearly had certain peers in mind, were knowledgeable of their experiences and even confessed to bullying their classmates. Their reasons are included in the table *Pupils' views on why some children are bullied* (page 34) and they have implications for preventative strategies and for inclusive practice, which is all too often associated with, and confined to, children with learning difficulties and is centred on disability rather than the celebration of individuality and tolerance of idiosyncrasies, difference or the unusual.

From the perspective of a preventative approach to bullying, eliciting the views of pupils is helpful and from them come implications for practice. For example:

- How will pupils develop a celebration of physical difference in a culture that appears to value limited bodily shapes and sizes?

- In an inclusive educational world how do we create a world that celebrates the many forms of intelligence that have been identified, yet few of which are formally assessed by the educational system?

- Should we teach children to be assertive, as opposed to aggressive, and how not to respond when other pupils appear to lose control?

A further complication is the cyclical nature of the problem in that once a pupil starts to bully another it can lead to retaliation, which attracts the bully further and the move to a bullying relationship begins and, before long, the role of the victim is institutionalized – everybody

Pupils' views on why some children are bullied (pupils aged between 9 and 11 years)	
Physical attribute	She is very skinny. He smells a bit and is dirty. He is fat. He comes from a different country. He's poor and he's got eczema. Their size or skin.
Learning problem	She can't read well. He is not very good at things. Some people can't do things as well as others. They are sometimes rubbish at work in class.
Emotional disposition or reaction	They get in moods easily. They are sensitive and don't stick up for themselves. They show off a lot and can get into a mood easily. He gets in big stress.
Retaliation	She is so bossy … she makes horrible remarks and is just a pain. He thinks he is better than people. They show off and lie and she 'dobs' on people. He picks on you first. She keeps on telling off people for been stupid and showing off.
Unclassified/various	Something about them that they don't like. For no reason. They don't like that person. A boy in our class gets picked on because he is new.

knows they get bullied. The answers to these problems are unlikely to come from perpetrators and those they pick on. Those who have been bullied extensively often show an unwillingness to report matters to teachers, occasionally deeming them unprepared to afford time and uninterested in their experiences (Lee, 1993). When a child has been repeatedly victimized, certain behaviours and attitudes tend to emerge which are inconsistent with their usual behaviours. Children are often too embarrassed and humiliated to report victimization, despite advice to tell, and initial support for victims may need to come from their peer group. The significance of the onlooker or bystander cannot be overstated.

Groups of pupils often adopt an informal hierarchical social structure within a class, with two or three pupils appearing to have power over a group and dominating the class, and the bullying is as much to do with membership, being 'in the gang', as with a perceived need to intimidate others. Pupils are looking to gain social power for themselves and, in doing so, exercise power over others. In a world of 'top dogs' and 'underdogs' the latter has little appeal for pupils. Therefore, maintaining the structure serves the interest of the majority, who fear becoming 'underdogs' themselves.

Within the social world of schools there are pupils who adopt a relatively pro-victim stance, especially evident amongst primary school pupils, and their sympathy is not linked with any negative experiences of their own nor any fear of bullies (Rigby and Slee, 1991). These are the pupils who find security in the knowledge that the world is a just place and they place emphasis on fairness. Such repositories of hope tend to decline, but not disappear, in older pupils where there is certainly a stronger tendency amongst pupils to locate blame with the victim rather than the bully (Hazler, Hoover and Oliver, 1992).

As indicated in the chapter on definitions, one noted subgroup is the 'provocative victim' who invites the attention of bullies and almost appears to need to be bullied. In their case, bullying may not always be something done *to* a person but that there is an interactive element, i.e. the victim contributes to the problem. They are characterized by being both anxious and aggressive, and often behave in ways that cause irritation and tension. They are occasionally hyperactive and have been noted as possessing problems with concentration. Their impact on class dynamics can be extensive as they possess an ability to provoke inappropriate behaviour amongst many children, perhaps the entire class. The consequence is that they lead to many pupils resorting to bullying behaviours when they might not normally be considered to be bullies. They are hard to like; even staff may find it hard to like them. As they have been instrumental in inviting the bullying, they also present specific challenges to the 'shared concern method' or 'no blame approach', discussed in detail later, in which attempts are made to help bullies acknowledge the hurt felt by their victims and act in alternative, more positive ways.

The Outlook for Those Who Are Picked On

Most, tragically not all, victims of school bullying do survive their experiences, but often carry their emotional scars for a lifetime. By the final year of secondary education, there is usually a decline in the number of bullying incidents, but victims know who the bullies are and seek to avoid them, tending to shun social contact, and an invisible boundary exists between what are now young adults. The bullying may well have left emotional scars, led to feelings about unhappiness at school that will stay into adulthood and may even remain for the rest of their life. It is hard not to conclude that they are unlikely to have achieved their full potential, as living in fear and being unhappy are not precursors to effective learning, and this proved to be the case for Edward.

ACTIVITY

Edward — case study of a victim of bullying

Participants: Staff

Time: 40 minutes

Equipment: Pen and paper.

This is not a fictional case but is a real account of a pupil from a senior class in a primary school. In small groups consider:

1   whether he is contributing to the bullying;

2   whether there should be pressure placed upon Edward to change his appearance or behaviour;

3   the strategies that need to be adopted to improve the situation for Edward and pupils like him.

Follow this with a full group discussion that shares conclusions and consider implications for practice.

EDWARD CASE STUDY

Question: 'Who picks on Edward?   Answer: 'Most of them do.'

Edward: Hell of a lot bully me and I get uptight about it and I get vicious. I'm the one that gets bullied. It's probably because they don't like me. I've hardly got any friends in school.

According to his peers what had led him to endure negative attention from others within the class was varied, but their responses could be categorized into four broad areas:

1 Background
His peers exploited features of his background, such as being an only child, living with his mother, no father in residence and being from a poorer home than many of his contemporaries

Sharon: It's where he comes from, where he lives, I don't know why but people just don't like him. I think he smells and things like that. Sometimes I'm a bit horrible to him but we all are — it's just a joke.

2 Ability
He was one of the weaker pupils academically in his class and was extracted for additional support with reading.

3 Appearance
Edward was also physically distinctive. He suffered from a skin complaint which, when added to his being overweight, meant that there were sufficient physical attributes for others to focus upon. He also was unkempt, presenting the image of not being able to look after himself or caring about how he appeared. His self-esteem seemed very low indeed.

4 Reaction

He was quick to anger, responded physically and sought to gain attention either positively or negatively or he became extremely upset and the tears flowed.

Derek: some friends of mine go round picking on him. They call him names like cos they think it's funny ... he goes off crying.

Edward conveyed an air of resignation and he painted a picture of isolation from almost the entire school community. When his classmates gathered in a circle he sat under a table away from the others, with no one commenting and considering his behaviour strange. He revealed that even very young pupils were not kind to him and 'dinner ladies' did little about him being bullied at lunchtimes. He was not alone in being over-weight and having learning difficulties, yet no one else appeared to possess the low status, which was coupled with a desire to draw attention to himself. He fulfilled the criteria that determined who will be selected for bullying (Whitney, Nabuzoka and Smith, 1992) in that he:

(a) possessed characteristics that distinguished him, physically and attitudinally, from others;
(b) was less socially integrated and therefore did not benefit from the protection a group can provide;
(c) responded aggressively and, therefore, may have provoked others to bully him.

Talking with his peers revealed little indignity or outrage about the victimization that he endured. In the opin-ion of some, Edward's demeanour meant that he almost invited negative attention and it was understandable that he was selected. Edward's characteristics were offered as justification for his selection.

Edward's story illustrates that particular pupils experience so much bullying that it becomes accepted, institu-tionalized even, at times, condoned by the social network of the class and, in this case, re-enforced by the attitude of the teacher. Children spoke of Edward with few endearing tones and he aroused little in the way of support or affection. Terms such as 'kid' and 'joke' were used as justification for actions against him, with an implied humour and lightness that Edward himself did not perceive nor share. There appeared to be a cyclical element in that he was selected for bullying because of physical or emotional attributes and, conse-quently, had developed such reactions as telling the teacher which, in turn, attracted more negative attention.

The case of Edward challenges two common features associated with bullying. First, that it is a playground phenomenon. Many of the bullying experiences of Edward happened in places other than the playground and at times other than recreation times. They stemmed from relationships that were part of everyday experi-ence in and out of the classroom. The second feature, the assumed covert nature of bullying, is also worthy of question. The bullying of Edward was manifest and the willingness of many pupils to talk about it affirmed that bullying was blatant, visible and, in his case, almost tangible. Being 'picked on' was such a dominant feature of Edward's classroom and school life that when asked to nominate children who get bullied he was the anticipated immediate first choice of his teacher. However, Mr Y made no mention of him and selected others that might fit the label before eventually citing him.

Mr Y: Now Edward is definitely a victim. He could wear a placard with that on and it wouldn't tell the children anything that they didn't know.

He described how even a new pupil to the school had selected Edward 'as someone he could victimize', implying he possessed transparent vulnerability. He elaborated by suggesting that Edward was a contributor to his situation and that his manipulative behaviour might be considered a form of bullying. His statement that some of his 'behaviours could be interpreted as bullying towards the other children' was based on the way that Edward demanded to be treated as a special case and that, to this end, he could be manipulative, even ensuring that 'teachers run around in circles to accommodate him'.

Edward's ragged appearance, poor co-ordination and reactive nature were factors that may have influenced him being bullied, but, because they generated little outrage, they were more difficult than factors such as race to address openly. His experiences of bullying were institutionalized within the classroom and play-ground relationships, and were taken for granted by the teacher, who exhibited an understanding as to why others might select him. Edward encountered few positive social experiences and little friendship, which meant that he was either tolerated at a distance or bullied.

Bullies

Before considering typologies of bullies it is important to reflect on the difference between an *aggressive bully* and an *aggressive child* since it is becoming more commonplace, especially in the media, to describe many forms of aggression as bullying. The major distinction centres on the fact that victims form a part of the process for the bullies, indeed there is almost a need to create a victim. Aggressive children are more random and not necessarily directing their aggression at specific individuals. Bullies possess power over specific victims or exploit a characteristic that is provocative. This distinction has implications for practice and policy in that approaches to dealing with bullying need to acknowledge that what has taken place was deliberate and controlled, whereas the aggressive child often has lost self-control.

Olweus (1999) suggests that we should view bullying as a subcategory of the broader aggressive behaviour and that violence forms another subcategory but both violence and bullying do not exist totally separately. Certain forms of bullying are violent and vice versa. However, *much that bullies do is not violent*, yet causes emotional hurt and much upset, for example, the occasional brawl in the playground would not qualify as bullying. Again there are implications for practice as there is a growing tendency to label all violence as 'bullying' which is a failure to acknowledge that bullying is more about establishing power over another person through hurt-ful, but not necessarily violent, means.

Bullies (Sometimes Called Aggressive Bullies)

The motivation to bully often puzzles the caring professions, and the behaviour of bullies can also arouse many emotions including feelings of hostility. It is important to understand why children are driven to bully others. Included in these are:

1   a desire for power, dominance over others and control;

2   a desire for social prestige that results from bullying, including seeking compensation for their own inadequacies as they crave social influence (Hazler, Hoover and Oliver, 1992). Bullies are often popular, especially in primary and the early years of secondary schooling. Even though their popularity can wane in the later secondary years, it does not sink to the low levels experienced by victims of bullying;

3 their home environment and upbringing which may include parent(s) permitting aggressive behaviour of the child towards peers and siblings, a lack of warmth and emotional attachment to parents (especially mother), unclear boundaries about behaviour or the use of aggressive behaviours by the parents;

4 a mixture of the above.

ACTIVITY

Working with parents

Participants: Staff

Time: 20–30 minutes

Equipment: Pen and paper.

Schools cannot change the backgrounds or upbringing of their pupils who bully, but they can influence and provide support for parents whose children may be bullying.

1 In small groups consider how awareness of factors such as:

  (a) desire for power;

  (b) desire for social prestige and status;

  (c) lack of warmth from, or licensed aggression by parents:

      can influence practice and the way that the school works with bullies and their parents;

2 Create a form of words that might be written into your anti-bullying policy.

3 Similarly, construct a similar statement for parents of the victims of bullying.

Meet again in the larger group and reflect on each statement and seek to construct a final form — it may have to be a compromise!

Amongst the challenges presented by the factors mentioned above are, in terms of control, power and prestige, how many opportunities do pupils have to be genuinely involved in decision-making and democratic processes and to exercise a degree of control in their life at school? Teachers relate to me that the whole culture of contemporary education sometimes appears to be predicated on a received curriculum and dictated from the powerful political centre. If that is the case, it is hardly surprising that anti-bullying initiatives have not always been greeted with enthusiasm and commitment in all schools. It is also understandable that where schools have set up pupils' councils and other forms of pupil involvement, including some with an anti-bullying focus, pupils who have bullied others are excluded. However, this represents one of the few opportunities for such pupils to observe or be part of decisions being made and acted upon in a non-aggressive manner.

Regarding the home environment and the lack of clarity and consistency in terms of parenting, it is clear that school can provide a compensatory environment. In order to do so the school needs to be clear and consistent in its application of anti-bullying strategies and the development of positive peer relationships. Unfortunately, as shown in the previous chapter, even at the level of terminology, the subject of bullying has not always been dealt with consistently in schools. At its most basic level, although staff may have differing views on what constitutes bullying, in theory, in practice pupils should not experience behaviour considered to be bullying in one classroom or year group and not in the next.

In contrast with the images of bullying as a bleak, out-of-sight, clandestine activity, children are often honest about their involvement in bullying and are prepared to talk about it. Given a context in which they are not being judged or punished they are able to talk with honesty and even tones of regret. There are those who simply confess and are even able to talk about their motives for doing so.

> Well if I'm honest yeah sometimes.

> When you start teasing him and everything he goes off in a huff. It is really funny.

Pupils who admit to bullying often give reasons for their actions and justify what has taken place, sometimes locating the fault with the victim or stating that the action was not deliberate and the hurt was unintentional.

> Kevin might cos he likes to think that we bully him, like when we get him.

> Adele, I used to always pick on her because Georgia kept really coming to me crying

> I don't mean to upset them, it's just that sometimes they get on my nerves.

Passive Bullies

'Passive' bullies (Besag, 1989) seek power for themselves but tend to adopt their role following initial action by aggressive bullies. They have been described as 'sad', having few endearing qualities, problems at home and a preparedness to accept blame without implicating the aggressive bully. They are likely to be less popular with peers than aggressive bullies but those closest to the bully might form cliques that insulate the group against unpopularity. They may not bully directly, but they preserve the informal social structure of the class.

Bully/Victims

One of the many faults with a simple bully and victim model is that it sometimes assumes that children are either victims, bullies or not involved, but research (Stephenson and Smith, 1987) has revealed that a number of children are both bullies and victims. It is tempting to speculate that the hostility directed by these children towards their victim is fuelled by their own experience of being victimized. Such a group, if it is a discrete group and not a manifestation of the idea that the more children become victims the more they are likely to bully, brings into question labels such as bully, victim and, even, bystander. It is essential not to lose sight of the concept that bullying is a behaviour that many pupils participate in to some extent and the use of labels such 'bully' and 'victim' can arouse many negative emotions. The idea of bully/victims draws into question that groups and subgroups are permanent and mutually exclusive (Lee, 1993). The triadic notion of bully, victim and non-involved could be a simplification and such descriptors may inhibit advancement in our understanding of bullying. Some children bully or are victimized in particular contexts, social groups or classes. An analysis of confidential telephone calls (La Fontaine, 1991) led to an observation that two-thirds of victims reported being bullied by more than one person and suggests that the children who carried out these acts were not all 'bullies' and that it did not reflect a permanent feature of their behaviour or character.

Bystanders

Bullies are often unwilling and victims unable to change, and therefore, amongst other factors, the significance of the bystander is in their potential to influence or bring the required change. A definition of the 'bystander' might be all those who are not bullies and victims of bullying but know that bullying is occurring, but the term is often associated with those who witness bullying yet appear to sanction it by their inertia in countering it. Those not directly involved often know what is happening and who is involved, and their indirect involvement has a capacity to impact upon their own lives and they may be said to be 'emotionally involved'. The bystander notion could also apply to staff who see bullying as inevitable, as in the case of Mr Y in the story of Edward, or parents who know that their children are involved as bullies, yet take no action or even condone it.

Bystanders have a critical role to play in the informal culture of schools and their views and insights would seem significant, especially if they are to be central to any intervention programme. Therefore, I have taken a broad definition of the term and, given that one of the principles of prevention is a belief in collaboration between all parties rather than the assumption that it is one person's responsibility to ensure an end to the bullying, the following section is subdivided into:

- Pupils;

- Staff;

- Parents.

Pupils

If involvement applies to witnessing events, then large numbers of pupils are implicated. Cullingford and Brown (1995) found that 50 per cent of pupils admitted to having seen bullying. Therefore, the distinctive feature that often leads to pupils being selected for picking on steps beyond the awareness of bullies alone and gives a message that many pupils know of the feature and it may become institutionalized. There develops a collective awareness about why the pupil has been selected and bystanders now become highly significant in the bullying relationship. Once that distinctive feature is institutionalized, the awareness of the social group may also have an impact on the behaviour of the victim, reinforcing the likelihood of further bullying. A once speculative act of bullying now becomes a major part the pupil's life in school and, perhaps, outside it. The status of 'victim' becomes established, as does increased feelings of lower social and academic self-worth amongst victims. A bystander is considered to be a person who does not become actively involved in a situation where someone else requires help (Clarkson, 1987). Someone requiring help implies knowledge of the need for help and there are those who:

1 know what is going on and who are involved but do nothing;

2 seek to exercise their power in the punishment of bullies and in doing so adopt methods that confirm that aggression and the abuse of power is a potent weapon;

3 disempower victims of bullying by over-protection – the 'rescuers';

4 despite knowledge of the potential impact of bullying on learning, the feelings of others and the school ethos, remain inert.

The notion of a bystander may be addressed in a number of ways. In working with pupils in schools, I have found the following story opens up the idea and develops the theme of involvement and the value that it may have for all parties. It is an adaptation of a tale sent to me by a friend from the USA who used it as part of a 'friendship week' which, in itself, is an idea that has merits as part of a policy promoting positive behaviour.

A STORY OF FRIENDSHIP

One day, when I was in secondary school, I saw a thin, smallish kid walking home from school, not my school but another school whose uniform I did not recognise. His name was Karl. It looked like he was carrying all of his school books. I thought to myself, 'Why would anyone bring home all their books on a Friday? He must be a real swot.'

I had quite a weekend planned with a party and a football game with my mates tomorrow afternoon, so I shrugged my shoulders and went on. As I was walking, I saw a bunch of kids running towards this kid, Karl. They ran at him, knocking all his books out of his arms and tripping him so he landed in the dirt. His glasses went flying, and I saw them land in the grass about 10 feet from him. He looked up and I saw this terrible sadness in his eyes. My heart went out to him. So, I ran over to him as he crawled around looking for his glasses and I saw that he was crying. As I handed him his glasses, I found myself saying, 'Those kids are real prats. They really should get lives.'

He looked up at me and simply said, 'Thanks!' A big smile came to his face. It was one of those smiles that showed genuine gratitude. I helped him pick up his books, and asked him where he lived. As it turned out, he lived near me, so I asked him why I had never seen him before. He said he had gone to private school before now. I have never talked to or really got to know a kid from a private school before. We talked all the way home and I carried some of his books.

He turned out to be okay, pretty cool in fact. I asked him if he wanted to play football on Saturday with my mates and myself. He said he would. We were around each other for most of the weekend and the more I got to know Karl, the more I liked him, and my friends all seemed to think the same of him.

Monday morning came and there was Karl with the huge stack of books again. I stopped him and said, 'You are really building some massive muscles with this pile of books every day!' He just laughed and handed me half the books.

Over the next four years, Karl and I became best friends, despite going to different schools. We began to think about university. Karl decided on Plymouth and I was going to Cardiff. I knew that we would always be friends, that the distance would never be a problem. he was going to be a doctor, and I was aiming to be a marine biologist.

Karl qualified highest in the whole of his year group at university which allowed me to carry on teasing him all the time about always being a swot and always carrying books. Because of his success he had to prepare a speech for the graduation and he invited me. I was so glad it wasn't me having to get up there and speak.

In his Graduation Day, I saw Karl. He looked great. He was one of those blokes that really changed and became the real Karl during his time at university. He had filled out and was much bigger now and actually looked good in glasses. He had more girlfriends than I had and all the girls seemed to love him. Frankly, sometimes I was jealous and today was one of those days. I could see that he was nervous about his speech. So, I smacked him on the back and said, 'Hey, big fella, you'll be great!' He looked at me with one of those looks (the really grateful one) and smiled. 'Thanks,' he said.

As he started his speech, he cleared his throat, and began. 'Graduation is a time to thank those who helped you make it through those tough years – your parents, your teachers, your siblings, but mostly your friends. I am here to tell all of you that being a friend to someone is the best gift you can give them. I am going to tell you a story'.

I just looked at my friend with disbelief as he told the story of the first day we met. He had planned to kill himself over the weekend. He talked of how he had cleaned out his locker so his Mum wouldn't have to do it later and was carrying his stuff home. He looked hard at me and gave me a little smile. 'Thankfully, I was saved. A friend saved me from doing the unspeakable.' I heard the gasp go through the crowd as this handsome, popular young man told us all about his weakest moment. I saw his parents looking at me and smiling that same grateful smile. Not until that moment did I realize its depth. Never underestimate the power of your actions. With one small gesture you can change a person's life – for better or for worse. You have that choice and that power.

Another way to work with bystanders is to consider the reasons or excuses that we are all capable of offering for why it is easier not to get involved in what is happening and remain a bystander. An aggressive exploratory act from a bully aims at establishing an imbalance of power, from which a victim is created and the role is sustained as much by the reactions of others as further attention from the bully. Not all onlookers are motivated in the same way. While there are those who watch and take no action, despite being upset, there are also those who appear indifferent, removed from the emotion. The role of bystanders in reinforcing any change of power or status is significant as they form key components of 'the audience'. Clarkson (1996) has developed a variety of categories of bystander that step beyond bullying and into all aspects of human relationships. They provide a framework which can be applied to the bullying phenomenon and which highlights that this third party, whether witnessing, colluding with or running away from bullying, has motive and reason behind his or her action. Before considering the framework it is important to emphasize how hard it is to be anything other than a bystander is and that the risks of intervention include loss of status, friendship and power, and also carries the risk of being bullied, but the alternative is licensing bullying and, eventually, the problem will return, often very personally. Clarkson's description of the various categories are in italics.

ACTIVITY

Bystanders — the keys to the solution?

Participants: Staff

Time: 50 minutes

Equipment: Pen and paper and distribute photocopies of **The various forms of bystander** (pages 44–5).

In smaller groups discuss:

1   Whether they are categories they recognize in the responses of their pupils?

2   Whether they are categories that they recognize in themselves?

3   How best to introduce these as discussion points with the class/school?

4   The implication for policy statements of a 'no such thing as a bystander' approach.

In a larger group, share innovative, plausible ways forward. The key objective will be how to generate a culture in which every pupil has the right to be safe in school and the responsibility to ensure the safety of others.

The various forms of bystander	
Wash hands **'It's none of my business'**	Victims request help but meet with a refusal to intervene. Responsibility is denied, mediation refused and victims may even be blamed.
Neutral **'I don't want to take sides'**	There is an appearance of fairness and being non-judgemental, although it is clear that there is a powerful party and a powerless one. Victims are left with a negative view of neutrality.
On the fence **'The truth lies somewhere in the middle'**	This bystander avoids making a judgement on the basis it is all a matter of perception — 'the fallacy of the mean'. It may be hard exactly to define bullying, but it is not as difficult to discern hurt and disempowerment.
Equilibrium **'I don't want to rock the boat'**	This is a fear of confronting the bullying. A superficial peace is maintained and emotions, especially those of the victim, are kept under the surface. Staff who have a good relationship with a pupil who bullies may be concerned that tackling the bullying will have a negative impact on their relationship.

The various forms of bystander – continued

Complicated 'It's more complex than it seems'	Complexity is no excuse. One ambition of this book has been to highlight the complexity of bullying, but this does not prevent intervention. Waiting for bullying to become a simple matter to understand or the truth to emerge invites permanent inertia.
Incomplete picture 'I don't have all the information'	Action is postponed on the basis of lacking a full picture or not knowing all who are involved. What is usually clear that is that someone has been hurt, bullying has taken place and waiting for full information may allow the situation to worsen.
History of hurt 'I don't want to get burned again'	Lack of action is based upon a bad experience while dealing with bullying in the past. Pupils will also employ this because of a previous negative experience. The thinking here is that what they tried in the past did not work, and here the need to have a variety of skills and intervention techniques is paramount.
Small fish 'My contribution won't make much difference'	The bystander does not intervene as they think it will not have any impact. It is not all self-deprecation and may simply be that they do not care enough. Often there are displays of guilt about a situation or demonstrations of helplessness.
Judge and jury 'I'm only telling the truth as I see it'	This is jumping to conclusions without speaking to key parties, recognition of the possibility of different perceptions or the complexity of the problem. They are remote and rely upon confidential information gathered from the non-involved.
Compliant 'I'm only following orders'	They claim to be subject to a more powerful authority and avoid difficult decisions though obedience. The victim is ignored because he or she brings an emotional element to what is resolved by re-ordained rules. Over-rigid adherence to policy, at local and national level, leads to the adoption of such a stance.
No business of mine 'I'm just keeping my own counsel'	Not getting involved because it is not immediately affecting them, until the bully turns their attention on to them. They may feel good about themselves as they reflect on the awful bullying that others are doing.
Their own fault 'Victim blaming'	Victims are seen as deserving all that comes to them. Sometimes this character colludes with bullies to ensure it or identify with the aggression yet remain guilt free. Even though provocative victims can appear to invite bullying, it does not follow that they have to be bullied or that is really what they needed.

Little is known about the long-term effects of witnessing bullying, and the emotional reactions of bystanders can range from amusement to sadness and guilt. Elliott (1997a) refers to 'bystander attitude' where an inability to take action, fearing reprisals from the bullies, disempowers those who witness events as well as the victims. Pupils, who are neither bullies nor victims, may be socially and emotionally involved, if not actively participating in the bullying process.

Supposedly non-involved pupils represent an under-explored area of the research, for their beliefs and ideas may be pertinent to the construction of relationships within schools and classrooms. As the table reasons why pupils feel that bullying is an important issue (page 47) suggests, they are very aware of the negative impact of bullying, indicating that the consequences for victims are long term as well as immediate and that the impact of bullying can be negative for the whole school. Their responses demonstrate maturity of thought and suggest that there are merits in class-based discussions on the subject. Five categories emerged:

1   Long-term, serious consequences for the victim – 'it could spoil your childhood life, which is important'.

2   Immediate physical and emotional outcome for the victim – 'people get put in hospital because of it'.

3   Description of the present/fatalistic – 'people don't get on with one another'.

4   Moral reasoning – 'you should not bully'.

5   Impact on school culture – 'it's not a good sign for the school'.

ACTIVITY

Pupils' views on the importance of dealing with bullying

Participants: Pupils

Time: 20–30 minutes

Equipment: Felt-tip pens, large sheets of paper or card.

Select a sample of the statements from **Reasons why pupils feel that bullying is an important issue** (page 47) and write them on large card or large sheets of paper. Display these for pupils to see from all parts of the room. In groups of three or five ask them to talk about the statements and answer the following questions:

1   Which statements do they find interesting or agree with?

2   What do those statements mean for the class or the school?

3   How do they think the important issue of bullying can be prevented?

Reasons why pupils feel that bullying is an important issue	
Long-term/serious consequences for the victim	If you don't try and deal with it they could live with it for the rest of their life. It could spoil your childhood life which is important. Children aren't going to enjoy school so they will learn less. You could grow up thinking that you are rubbish. It can ruin lives. It upsets people so that they don't want to go to school. Some people commit suicide.
Immediate physical/emotional outcome	People get put in hospital because of it. People get hurt. People get upset.
Description of the present/fatalistic	Quite a lot of people get bullied. People don't get on with one another. It happens a lot.
Moral reasoning	I think bullying is not very nice. You should not bully. It's horrible for children who get bullied.
Impact on school culture	Bullying might get worse. All the little children will think bullying is a good thing to do. All children have to try to get on. People are falling out too often so it makes it harder for the teacher to control you. It's not a good sign for the school.

'The behaviour of everyone in the classroom or school in which a problem occurs influences and is influenced by that problem behaviour'

(Molnar and Lindquist, 1990).

Preventative techniques in anti-bullying policies usually focus on those more directly involved, i.e. victims or bullies, and not enough emphasis is placed upon the school as a whole. One reason for analysis stepping beyond the bully and victim model is that pupil behaviour does not exist in isolation and has the potential to be perceived differently. Human beings who share a common physical environment may interpret the meanings of events within that environment very differently for reasons influenced by social factors (Molnar and Lindquist, 1990). This is a key tenet of the ecosystemic approach in which problem behaviours are perceived as part of the wider social setting in which they occur and the behaviour of everyone in the classroom or school influences and is influenced by it. It is an acknowledgement of the power of all pupils to influence change and that they are far from being 'non-involved' as they possess both considerable power and responsibility.

Teachers

Given the potential impact of bullying on pupils' self-esteem, learning, classroom friendships, long-term relationships and even the desire to continue with life, teachers' knowledge, attitude and action would seem significant, if not paramount. They possess power to support pupils, punish them, organize the classroom and influence, even determine, the classroom climate.

Pervin and Turner (1994) explored the views of teachers on bullying and compared data from pupils and their teachers from a single comprehensive school. They concluded that teachers underestimate the extent of bullying, despite it being extensively reported to them by pupils. It is clear that pupils believe that teachers *occasionally* intervene in bullying, while the majority of teachers believe they *always* intervene and it appears that there is a need to relate to pupils what is being done and how it is being monitored. Similarly, it is important that pupils and their parents keep staff in schools informed of progress or otherwise. School staff need to know what works and when interventions need modification or abandoning. Boulton (1997) has tentatively concluded that teachers feel a responsibility to prevent bullying, yet possess somewhat low levels of confidence in dealing with it.

'Most teachers are only aware of a fraction of the bullying which may be going on' (Smith and Sharp, 1994) and teachers may remain unaware of the bullying because of the conspiracy of silence that bullying encourages or is allowed to encourage. There are often references to the need to break a code of secrecy that surrounds bullying, yet it may well be that it is only a secret to teachers within the school, forming part of what Blatchford (1996) has termed the 'child-governed culture of the playground, alien to that of adults and mysterious to them'. However, in my research into primary classes, teacher nominations of those who are involved match those of pupils. They knew the children when they were in earlier classes and witnessed the development of social relationships, both negative and positive, as they progressed through the school. Secondary schools do not generate similar confidence, which is not surprising given the number of different teachers and configurations of class groups that pupils experience in a week. The role of the tutor is crucial and tutorial groups become essential to finding out about and acting upon incidents.

Parents

Books on bullying written with a readership of parents in mind are mainly advisory and rarely contain accounts of parents' experiences or relate their advice to the context of school. Pervin's (1995) research, based in a single case study secondary school, concluded that almost one in five parents who visited the school on bullying issues felt let down. The disappointment was founded on not knowing who to contact or receiving unsympathetic responses from teachers. More than a third of parents of pupils who had been bullied were asked by their own children not to contact the school. They had acquiesced to the wishes of their children, trusting in their children's ability to cope, which, given that they had resorted to telling their parents, was a dubious strategy. The implications for policy here are ensuring that there are clear contact points – named people with telephone contact numbers or e-mail addresses – and, although it is difficult to mention bullying on such occasions, on induction days or evenings make sure that parents and new pupils know of those key contacts points.

Given the emotions that a child being bullied or being involved in incidents in any way can excite, it is essential that schools and parents have a clear comprehension of each other's stance on the subject and how incidents will be managed. As highlighted in the table, *Parents' views on teachers and pupils* (page 50), parents, like other parties, do not possess a single view on bullying, nor is it to be expected that there should be a single parental perspective. They need the opportunity to make their views known and to share their understanding with other parents as well as staff and children. Lack of consistency and clarity on anti-bullying policy can lead to an impression that there is inertia or, worse still, that staff condone bullying.

Some activities in this book can easily be adapted to provide ideas for parent workshops that discuss bullying and render explicit what is implicit. One of the ways that I have been involved with schools is in such workshops on anti-bullying approaches and two impressions have been left. First, in asking me to work with them, these were the schools which needed me least for they are open and are prepared to admit that bullying might take place and that the best way to tackle it is in an informed and supportive manner. Second, the parents who attend such workshops are mainly those who know or believe that their children are being bullied and use the event to complain, seek advice or meet others in a similar situation. The school which looks to involve more than the bullies and victims in bringing reconciliation, and which forges genuine parent partnership schemes, is also likely to find interest in building positive relationships and anti-bullying strategies from a variety of sources, not just those who feel frustrated or disenfranchised. As we advise pupils to make bullying less secretive, parents might also be encouraged to offer their views, especially given that all parties may exist in a world of *presumed shared understanding*. Just as assumptions that we live in a world that is outraged about bullying are occasionally countered by a member of staff's view that interest in bullying is yet another example of overload in a system by which the teacher, him or herself, felt bullied, so too there will be the occasional parent's perception of the contemporary concern surrounding bullying as another 'politically correct' matter which will eventually return to the background of social issues.

ACTIVITY

What action parents think staff and pupils should take

Participants: Staff

Time: 30 minutes

Equipment: Copies of **Parents' views on teachers and pupils** will need to be photocopied and distributed to groups.

Staff in small groups consider each statement and respond to:

1 Whether such a comment would be valid in their context?

2 What are the implications for working with parents?

In the full group, share responses and how these will have an impact on practice.

Parents' views on teachers and pupils

Parents on ...	Quotation
Teachers	The teachers know all the children better than us parents. They can see the bullies in action in classes.
	They seem to wait and see how the situation develops instead of taking immediate action.
	A lot of the time I feel they listen but don't always act. Also teachers tend to act on the parent's complaint but not always when children go to them for help.
	My experience is that teachers generally deal well with such incidents, when they become aware of them.
	The child in question was only isolated from other children for one playtime.
	I would be rather concerned that there would be an awful lot of just what you would term as natural life could be lumped under that same heading and given more importance and more emphasis than perhaps it should.
Pupils	Children need to know to bully is wrong and not allow it to go on around them, to support other students and to tell.
	If they did no teasing or bullying it won't get done to them.
	The older children could be made aware of school procedure for bullies and they themselves could isolate the person.
	Some children need to have more patience and understanding of others' problems. Not tease if others are fat, spotty or poorly dressed.
	I feel that it should be known that a child can help by informing someone and not get into trouble by doing so or be ignored.
	To be aware of what is going on around them and also to have the courage in certain circumstances to not go along with the crowd but to be prepared to take positive action.
	We have told her if somebody attacks you they must expect you to defend yourself, so do it if you are defending yourself – you are allowed to defend yourself ... you must be prepared to defend yourself because, at that point, nobody is.
	I think they shouldn't stand outside. I think they should speak up and say 'oi' to the person but I don't think children do.
	Just stay out of the way, walk away from it, it's not worth it.
	I have told him to tell his teacher, not to do anything, walk away.

Parents find out that their children are victims of bullying through being told directly by them or noticing distress or uncharacteristic behaviour. As they listen to the experiences of their children a diverse range of experiences often unfolds. Parents have reported to me that the spectrum of experience ranged from sexual interference to aggressive tackling in football and, in a few cases, they were aware that something was amiss and reported it to the school which undertook to observe matters and relayed results. On occasions, little was found to substantiate the suspicions of those parents.

Advice for children to tell teachers abounds in literature produced to support pupils, but for some pupils it proves almost impossible to tell anyone. If changes in a child's behaviour, disposition or attitude are the means by which bullying becomes conspicuous, it is more likely that parents will be the initial inspiration for action and their role at the beginning of intervention is crucial.

Among the ways that parents came to know that something was wrong were:

■ silence where there was normally a talkative child;

■ inability to sleep;

■ reluctance to attend school;

■ nightmares;

■ a form of physical reflection of an emotional upheaval, e.g. 'tummy aches';

■ untypical aggression shown in the family, often towards a younger sibling;

■ being informed by other children (usually siblings);

■ a radical change in behaviour, such as a normally happy child becoming sullen;

■ when the situation had become sufficiently serious that the victim retaliated and then found her/himself in trouble with teachers;

■ unusual statements, such as one mother who I worked with reported that her daughter uncharacteristically stated that 'I don't want to eat pudding tonight because I'm fat' providing the key clue that something was wrong in her daughter's life.

In summary, there are four areas that parents and staff can work together on in identifying symptoms of bullying. First, there is *absence from school* through truanting, being unwilling to go to school or suddenly developing an 'illness'. Second, there are *problems with going to or returning from school* such as being frightened to walk, changing their route or asking to be driven to school when they are usually content to walk, plus damage to clothes, property or school work or with unexplained scratches, bruises or cuts. They also return from school in an unusually hungry state or ask for money, as the bully has taken their dinner money. Third, there are *problems at school* such as beginning to underachieve in school or being involved in aggressive behaviour. Finally, there are *changes in habits or behaviour* such as becoming surly or aggressive to other members of the family or becoming withdrawn, distressed, anxious, lacking confidence which can lead to further serious problems including stammering, not eating, threatening suicide, crying at night or nightmares and beginning to steal. Agreement between staff and parents to inform each other about concerns can only enhance the chances of early intervention and the development of a united, supported and consistent response. When working with parents, staff need to emphasize that many of the above symptoms could indicate other concerns or they could mean nothing at all. For example, a change in route could simply be that a child is bored with their usual route.

Noting that their child might be being bullied often leads parents to react with understandable panic. The following advice is designed to emphasize calm and consider what part they might play in bringing resolution.

- Count to one hundred – don't act in haste.

- Alert the school and arrange an appointment to visit – it may be class teacher, head of year, tutor. Think about whether your child's presence at the meeting will help.

- Contacting the school makes the issue more public and this, in itself, can help stop bullying, but your child may fear that it will make things worse.

- Gather as much information as possible and your own thoughts. Write it down. Do not assume you have the truth – all you have is an account.

- You may hear that your child is no 'angel', may contribute to the problem or even may have started the bullying. This does not alter your purpose and that is to contribute towards an end of the bullying.

- Try to avoid anger – there is enough aggression already.

- Ask what the school policy is (have you got a copy?).

- Protection for victims by adults may be required, but this is not a long-term solution.

- Encourage the child to approach a teacher with whom they feel comfortable.

- Try to avoid holding family discussions within the hearing of the child.

- In your talks with your child, emphasize that there is nothing wrong with them.

- Maintain a sense of hope and, however hard it may seem, a sense of humour without undermining the seriousness of the situation.

- Encourage activities that help the child to forget the bullying.

- Try to build their self-confidence.

- Maintain communication with the school, even if the bullying stops – they need to know that what they did has worked.

Working in partnership with parents may add a layer to the complex problem of preventing bullying incidents, but the benefits of a policy of full involvement will serve to help eliminate the secrecy sometimes associated with the phenomenon and help to alleviate the tensions and stresses that misunderstanding can generate.

CHAPTER 4

What is needed in an anti-bullying policy

This chapter offers a practical and thorough guide to generating an anti-bullying policy. It facilitates an examination of the ethos of the school and suggests a menu of items that a school can personalize into its own policy. The outcome of the activities is a school policy that many know about, feel ownership of and reflects the values of a broad range of staff and pupils.

In part, bullying in schools stems from external forces and the wider social problems and attitudes and, therefore, long-term answers will include a broader, societal approach that considers areas such as community education, parenting skills and the development of inclusive cultures. However, schools possess the capacity to make a difference and those who see them as institutions whose efficacy can be measured by narrow examination and test results deny the more meaningful potential that they also have to generate social change and nurture tolerant attitudes. They are powerful forces in determining the experiences of their pupils and possess a capacity to ignore, foster or condone bullying. Their policy and practice in countering bullying is significant and it follows that failure to do so would mean that they are a *contributory cause* of bullying.

The Importance of Taking Action against Bullying

Throughout this book is a commitment to action being taken to counter bullying and to help ensure that schools are safe places for all their pupils. What follows are a number of reasons why schools should take action, but they are not the only ones:

- Bullying has an impact on learning.
- Bullying is an enduring problem in schools.
- Many bullies end up with a criminal conviction.
- The emotional scars for both victims and bystanders can last a lifetime.

- Children who are repeatedly victimized resort to drastic means to escape, including suicide.

- Bullies are eventually disliked by the majority of their peers.

- Parents often do not know how to intervene in bullying situations, therefore the experience of their children is overlooked.

- Bullying occurs extensively in certain schools.

- The majority of bullying occurs in or near to school or on the journey to school.

- Victims are often unlikely to report bullying.

The Whole-School Policy

If all or most of the above are true then countering bully is a serious matter that demands thoughtful attention through a policy that is read, understood and known by all. A policy will mention the *proactive approaches* to countering bullying, i.e. those that aim to create the structures and climates in school that make bullying anathema and set a tone and raise awareness; therefore they are difficult to evaluate in terms of their efficacy, but are essential in creating an anti-bullying culture. It will also make explicit the *reactive strategies*, i.e. what will be the school's response if bullying is found to have occurred.

Prevailing climate and ethos in a school are significant factors in determining whether bullying is countered effectively. Lane (1989) suggests that 'there are high and low bullying schools' and that policy decisions have an impact on levels of bullying and that schools have a key role to play in promoting or combating bullying. Schools rely on structures based upon status differentials and hierarchical divisions of power, and these structures, in themselves, are vulnerable to the misuse of that power and create climates in which it becomes difficult for victims to seek help. It might be seen as an admission of weakness. An anti-bullying school is one in which teachers do not ridicule or make negative comments about any pupils, especially the more vulnerable. 'Asymmetry of power' focuses not only on relationships between pupils but, in a broader context, such a concept applies to the use and abuse of power within an institution and the methods employed to involve staff and pupils in decision-making processes.

Despite recent emphasis on examination achievement and the publication of league tables, parents continue to see their child's safety and happiness as the principal determinants of whether a school is successful. If a child does not feel safe at school, it can have an impact on everything that goes on in their life. Rightly or wrongly, certain schools acquire a reputation for tolerating bullying or appearing to be inactive in countering it and this reputation is often common knowledge amongst the pupils and beyond into the wider community. While sometimes such an image is unjustified, it is hard not to conclude that in the time that a school develops a public reputation for being 'unsafe' or 'tough', many victims have suffered in silence and without resolution of their difficulties.

Once a school gains a reputation for being active in countering bullying, safe for all children and having, as some might say, a 'zero tolerance' attitude, bullies are provided with a platform which they can challenge. Therefore, it is important that the school maintains consistency and monitors the experiences of pupils. They need to know that the policy will be reviewed and they may take a part in the process. Having used the phrase 'zero tolerance' I feel compelled to express concerns about it as tolerance is an essential feature of a caring society and tolerance of individual difference underpins so many approaches to dealing with bullying. It is important to be *informed, clear and consistent* in an anti-bullying policy and, whilst the school will not condone or licence bullying, to say that 'zero-tolerance' exists states a position that is rigid and intolerant, not flexible or needs-driven. Given the problems of definition and interpretation of bullying, 'zero-tolerance' seems to be a strategy fraught with the risk of erroneous blame.

Devising a policy is not a simple process. At its most basic it is a series of statements expressing what the school will do about bullying and offering pupils and parents advice. It is written by an interested or willing volunteer and reviewed as part of the annual review of documentation. It reflects the values of the teaching staff or perhaps just senior management. At its most complex it is a long-term, sophisticated examination that steps beyond the bullying issue to matters of personal values and promotes tolerance, respect and a concern for the well-being and rights of others. It demands flexibility to accommodate a variety of needs and to address a variety of audiences. The policy forms a cornerstone of any anti-bullying strategies whether it is a discrete policy or one that exists within a broader behaviour policy or as part of the school community's responsibilities to help form positive relationships. To help tackle the challenge of writing policy there are three activities that provide a framework that informs the process. *Preparing to write an anti-bullying policy* (page 56) deals with fundamental questions about the nature of the policy that need to be answered at the outset. Schools have an impact on bullying and the attitude and knowledge of leaders and managers within the school can also have an impact. An examination of the ethos and how it is perceived by all staff is a way of beginning the journey of constructing policy and practice. *The pro-bullying and the anti-bullying school* activity (page 57) takes a look at the school itself and differences between 'pro' and 'anti' bullying schools. It is an open, exploratory discussion on what difference a school can make and, having reflected on those deliberations, *the components of an anti-bullying policy* (pages 58–9) directly inform the content and is the final element prior to publication of the document.

ACTIVITY

Preparing to write an anti-bullying policy

Participants: Staff

Time: 40–50 minutes

Equipment: Pen and paper and photocopies of **Preparing to write an anti-bullying policy: key questions** (page 56).

In small groups consider the following questions and write responses in the space provided in each section. Get together in the larger group, share ideas and consider the implications before moving on to consider the policy itself.

Preparing to write an anti-bullying policy: key questions

What are the core values of the school?
The 'mission' statement would incorporate a wide range of considerations: e.g. statements about encouraging friendship, support and co-operation, pupil involvement, how a safe environment might be created.

Should the policy be self-standing, i.e. about the school's approach to dealing with bullying?
Should it form part of the wider policy on behaviour in the school? Will it 'lock into' other policies and approaches?

How far is policy on paper seen around the school as a policy in practice, including staff–pupil and staff–staff relationships?

Who will be involved in policy generation?
If a school embraces an approach that gives power to pupils, perhaps they should be involved in the policy formulation. The process of creating policy, and the understanding of it by all key parties, would appear to be crucial in determining the efficacy of that policy. It is important to differentiate between policy which is created 'top down' and that which is generated 'bottom up', the former being the creation of senior managers and the latter involving staff (and pupils) at all levels which reflects democratic attitudes towards sharing power, notions of ownership and common values.

What are the feelings of the staff?
Policy and practice devised because of external pressure can often be distinguished from a policy that is based on a conviction from within the school that bullying must be tackled.

Will it incorporate awareness-raising and preventative approaches as well as reactive elements?
This will have implications for professional development sessions and deciding who will be involved, i.e. will all staff be involved, will governors be invited and what awareness-raising will pupils and parents require?

ACTIVITY

The pro-bullying and the anti-bullying school

Participants: Staff

Time: 40 minutes

Equipment: Pen and paper and copies of **The pro-bullying school and the anti-bullying school** (page 57).

In small groups ask staff to complete their responses to the following:

1 What are the key features of a pro-bullying school (features that license, nurture, encourage, promote or permit bullying)?

2 What are the key features of an anti-bullying school (features that inhibit or prevent bullying)?

3 Which elements of the pro-bullying school exist in your school?

4 What changes need to be made to become an anti-bullying school?

Share findings in the whole group with a focus on the implications for the policy.

The pro-bullying school and the anti-bullying school		
Issue	Pro-bullying	Anti-bullying
Rules, traditions, practices and procedures		
The structure		
Resources		
The curriculum		
The relationship between school and community		
Staff relationships (sarcasm, humiliation, unpleasant nicknames)		
Staff–pupil relationships		
School activities, e.g. assemblies, camps, sports days, etc.		
Other		

The preparation and the thinking behind the policy is now complete and it remains to address the document itself and what it will contain.

ACTIVITY

The components of an anti-bullying policy

Participants: Staff

Time: 60+ minutes

Equipment: Pen and paper and copies of **What might go into an anti-bullying policy** (see below).

Distribute to small groups and read the following instructions to them:

'This is a checklist of elements that might form part of an anti-bullying policy. In groups annotate those that you see as essential "E", those which are desirable "D" and those which are not necessary or appropriate "N". Space has deliberately been left for any additional information you believe should be added.'

Reconvene the larger group and determine that those deemed 'essential' by most groups will definitely be the policy and those considered 'not necessary' will be omitted. In the case of the 'desirables' further discussion will be needed perhaps in differently constituted small groups. This time they must be either E or N. While this may be a long process the final product involves staff professionally, makes values explicit and provides a sense of consensus.

What might go into an anti-bullying policy		
No.	Component	E, D, N
1	A definition of bullying and perhaps a statement that highlights that no given definition can be perfect or all embracing.	
2	A clear statement of the school's approach or stance on bullying.	
3	Reference to some of the leading myths and misconceptions such 'it is part of growing up' or 'boys will be boys'.	
4	A description of the policy-generating process and how the ideas enclosed were generated. It would also include a statement on who has been involved in creating the policy — the more diverse and all-encompassing this is, the more credence the policy possesses.	
5	Clear statement of the audience(s) or distribution list that the policy addresses: staff, pupils, parents and governors? What are the implications for these groups and what roles might they play?	
6	A statement that highlights that bullying is a rights issue and consequently a responsibility issue.	
7	An elaboration on what responsibilities members of the school's community have to ensure the success of the policy (who constitutes 'members' is the crucial matter here).	
8	Advice for those who are picked on.	

| **What might go into an anti-bullying policy – continued**			
No.	Component		E, D, N
9	Advice for bystanders.		
10	Clear outline of actions/sanctions for perpetrators.		
11	A statement which highlights that pupils will be listened to and their concerns will be taken seriously.		
12	Clear statements that inform children who to tell and how to convey that information.		
13	How will information be recorded?		
14	An outline of what the school has put into place as preventative approaches.		
15	An outline of what strategies are in place to deal with bullying (and perhaps other forms of peer conflict).		
16	A statement of how information will be recorded and from whom it will be gathered.		
17	Advice for parents on how to recognize bullying and what action to take if their child **has been bullied**.		
18	Advice for parents on how to recognize bullying and what action to take if their child **has bullied**.		
19	Advice for parents on how to recognize bullying and what action to take if their child **knows of or has seen bullying**.		
20	How parents can help staff and children at the school.		
21	Named person or people, contact addresses and key information on who can help all parties involved.		
22	What professional development linked to the policy will take place and who will be able to take advantage of it.		
23	Useful books, websites that offer advice on dealing with bullying.		
24	How and when the policy will be monitored, reviewed and evaluated.		
25	Whether outside agencies are involved. If so which ones and how are they involved?		
26	Whether awareness-raising takes place through the formal curriculum and in what way.		
27	How new members of staff are informed about it (at interview or soon after?).		
28	The financial implications of the policy.		
29	....		
30	....		

Unfortunately schools may be compelled to conceive of the policy in a negative framework, such as in anticipation of a forthcoming inspection and having to comply with external pressures to deliver policy, which is hardly the basis for informed and reflective judgement. There has also been pressure on schools to link bullying with wider discipline issues, which has come through the OFSTED inspection guidance and government documents that have isolated bullying as an issue that should be countered in that 'all schools must have a clear discipline policy ... this policy must include strategies to prevent bullying' (DfEE, 1998).

Most pupils strongly believe in fairness and welcome anti-bullying policies based upon treating others with care and respect. However, pupils are more likely to support a policy when they have been directly involved in determining it and they feel a sense of ownership of it. Staff need to be sensitive to potential ethical problems such as ensuring that information from pupils will not cause them to lose status in their peer group. Where appropriate, confidentiality needs to be maintained in order for the programme to be viewed by the pupils as credible. It is extemely important that they learn the difference between 'dobbing' and 'reporting'. 'Dobbing' occurs when pupils tell about an inappropriate act with the purpose of getting another pupil into trouble. 'Reporting' happens when a student tells to protect the safety of another student. Once pupils have an understanding of the difference between the two, reporting bullying incidents assumes much less of a social taboo.

One way of raising awareness and promoting positive pupil relationships has been the idea of a pupil charter that is embedded in ideas of pupil rights and responsibilities:

Rights such as to:

- *feel* safe at school as well as to *be* safe;

- be free from insult and negative teasing;

- be able to associate with other people for friendship;

- feel that possessions are secure.

Therefore, the responsibilities are to ensure:

- the safety of others;

- the security of their possessions;

- freedom from teasing and name-calling.

Working with pupils through such activities as 'True for you?' p. 61, it is apparent that most are outraged at the unfairness of bullying, as well as occasionally feeling helpless about being able to do anything about it. It is useful to help pupils to make their views known and to share them with others including staff.

Throughout this chapter emphasis has been mainly upon the creation of a policy *document*, the physical manifestation of the attitudes and approaches and procedures adopted by staff and perhaps children in the school. It is an expression of values as well as the direction that the school follows. Following the construction of the policy there remains the problem of its distribution and ensuring that its wisdom does not become just another piece of paper sent home or placed in a file. Workshops, websites, assemblies, classroom and playground activities will all contribute to rendering it *live* and to raising awareness. An anti-bullying policy contributes towards ensuring a safe, happy learning environment for all and will include ideas and techniques that let people know how bullying is dealt with through raising awareness and what will happen if it occurs.

ACTIVITY

'True for you': statements on bullying for pupils' consideration

Participants: Pupils

Time: 60+ minutes

Equipment: You will require either photocopies of the **True for you?** list (see below) or sets of copies of each statement reproduced on laminated card.

There are many ways in which they can be used:

1   Pupils are invited, in groups, to consider whether they believe each statement is true or false. Older pupils may prioritize them in order of nearest to truth and younger pupils can place them in order of truth. After 15 minutes the facilitator invites comparison of lists and the reasoning behind it.

2   One way of providing a focus is to say that the top four choices will form part of the pupils' charter or the school anti-bullying policy.

3   Another way is to consider them in circle time with emphasis on two questions. First, what do they think of the statements and, second, what needs to be done as a result of the discussion?

True for you?

- I do not have to put up with bullying.
- It is okay to tell on bullies.
- It is not okay to bully.
- Bullying hurts my body and my feelings.
- I am an individual.
- I respect people's possessions.
- We are all different, yet share a great deal.
- I have rights and with them come responsibilities.
- There are people I can ask for help.
- There are things I can do to stop bullying.
- I can play safely without hurting others.
- You have to be a friend to have a friend.
- I am responsible for my own actions.
- I can help make our class a bully-free zone.

CHAPTER 5

What Might Be Put in Place

This chapter informs the reader on a variety of approaches that will be needed to underpin the policy. It looks at what can be achieved through the curriculum, gathering data and supporting and enhancing the skills of mealtime-assistants. It also considers how identified bullying can be dealt with in line with school policy and the values that it embraces.

There are a range of preventative anti-bullying strategies available to schools covered in this chapter and they take two forms. First, there are those which *raise awareness* and provide arenas in which pupils and staff can begin to understand bullying in all its complexities. Their impact is impossible to measure, but they say a great deal about how seriously the school and the staff take the subject and how empowering and imaginative they are being. All the activities included in the previous chapter are of that type. Second, there are those which aim to *manage events* after the bullying has taken place. Be they punitive or counselling based, these approaches also serve to reflect on the school culture and their place in school tells those who are bullied that they will find support and those who bully that their behaviour is not being licensed. They testify to the seriousness with which bullying is taken and reflect upon the school culture, therefore their very existence is preventative. The first part of this chapter looks at the proactive methods that raise awareness and develop empowering cultures.

Awareness-raising

Through the Curriculum

Methods of countering bullying through the curriculum are divided in two. First, there are those that raise awareness and seek to explore the potential of the informal pastoral curriculum, the 'affective' curriculum. Aimed at the promotion of democratic values in the school, the more informal curriculum is an essential part of any preventative strategy. Emphasis is placed on the establishment of a forum for decision-making within the classroom that permits pupils to make important decisions and to use power constructively. Included in these are co-operative group work, which seeks to enhance relationships and involve all pupils in working together as teams (Cowie, 1995), and circle time. Second are those approaches that seek to integrate the topic of bullying and related issues with the subject-based curriculum. Here are some examples:

History provides an opportunity to consider those who have abused power or have championed the cause of others and not remained bystanders.

Drama offers the chance to enact bullying incidents and their resolution or otherwise (Casdagli and Gobey, 1990). This subject explores emotions or, through role play, develops techniques that prove effective in standing up to bullying.

Mathematics is a chance to explore experiences of pupils through questionnaires. The data can be analysed and recorded graphically and is created, owned and understood by pupils (see *Gathering Data*).

Art provides a vehicle for expressing feelings or experiences that sometimes cannot be conveyed in words or creating anti-bullying posters.

Music again presents the chance to express feelings through music, including generating 'bullying raps'.

A powerful exploratory vehicle for the subject is children's fictional literature, of which there has been a proliferation in recent years (Stones, 1998). 'Bibliotherapy' has been heralded as having the potential to equip pupils with strategies for contemplation and, perhaps, practice (Oliver, Young and LaSalle, 1994). It has both disadvantages and advantages, and highlights the importance of planning and linking the methods to the school context.

On the negative side:

■ there has been little research into the efficacy of such approaches in changing the attitudes and values of pupils;

■ where the focus is on the *message* of a book rather than the book itself, it could inhibit the sense of reading just for the pleasure of it.

On the positive side:

■ it is a therapeutic element, as it can lead to a form of emotional release;

■ it permits identification with characters involved and insights into associated problems and dilemmas.

Poetry is among the many areas of the curriculum that provide an arena in which relationship issues can be explored and the value of acrostic poems to explore feelings and share understanding cannot be overstated. The following acrostic poem was created by a group of teaching assistants and support workers whom I worked with in a special school for pupils with emotional difficulties. Arriving at the final product took several hours as the discussion ranged around a wide variety of significant topics and the process that led to the poem was an example of a team working closely, agreeing and disagreeing, responding to the values and opinions of others and, finally, arriving at a statement that was a compromise but which they all felt some ownership. In many ways it resembled the process of good policy-generation.

Bullying and Teasing in Schools

Being unusual sometimes means
Understanding is hard it seems,
Little or large, fat or thin,
Liked a lot, I've never been,
You never ask me how I feel,
I feel hurt, sad and alone,
Now I've found a way to go,
Get in my shoes then you'll know.

Gathering Data

Countering the climate of secrecy that can, but does not have to, accompany bullying includes the idea that schools, and classes within those schools, carry out pupil surveys to determine levels of bullying and the nature of the pupil experience so that they generate an understanding of the problem. Such surveys serve not only to provide information, but also give a message that bullying is being considered in an open and informed manner. Encouraging pupils to undertake interviews or questionnaires with their peers links research into bullying with motivating pupils to take action. One of the many benefits of such research is that it takes place in a real context, as it is about *their* school and the experiences of *their* friends and colleagues, and not someone else's synthesis or view on data across a variety of schools. Such surveys help to inform on levels of bullying. For example, they could provide comparisons of experiences of pupils in Year 5 with those in Year 6. However, they do carry with them a number of questions that need consideration, e.g.:

- Confidentiality – will names or other forms of identification be included and, if so, what will be the effect of this on data provided by the pupils?

- Younger pupils or those with literacy difficulties – are there alternatives such as pictorial methods that can be used or would interviews prove to be a suitable method?

- Validity – if questionnaires are employed to measure the before and after effects on incidences levels of a particular intervention, cautions about whether incidence levels are the best way of measuring bullying need to apply.

- Whose question are they?

- How are they generated?

In one secondary school in which I undertook a research project I was invited by a group of Year 9 pupils to work with them on an anti-bullying project. My role was not that of adviser on the bullying matters; I was there to support the development of their questionnaire on bullying throughout the year group. After a little advice and several drafts we arrived at the document included in this book (pages 65–6). Not everyone would agree with particular phrases or the exclusion or inclusion of certain questions, but the power of this questionnaire lies in its ownership and administration. As important as the findings, was the empowerment of pupils to find out for themselves what others experienced and thought. The validity of findings, like any form of research, needs to be questioned and the students themselves were aware that responses were directed at, and in language familiar to, their peers. My involvement was technical and supportive whereas the research itself was administered and analysed by the students. The results led to discussion undertaken in circle time and a meeting with senior Year 9 staff to consider findings.

Bullying Questionnaire

A) ABOUT YOU – (No names are required but we would like some information)

I am (please circle)   Female   Male   Class ....

B) WHAT IS BULLYING?

Please write down what you think bullying is.

Bullying is

....

....

C) BEING BULLIED

Have you ever been bullied in this school? (please circle)   Yes   No

If you said 'Yes', in what way(s) were you bullied?

....

....

....

Were you bullied in any other school? (please circle)   Yes   No

If you answered 'No' go on to Section D.

If you said 'Yes', in what way(s) were you bullied?

....

....

....

Who did you tell? (please tick)

a) Parent(s)   e) Head of Year

b) Brother or sister   f) Friend

c) No one   g) Anyone else? ....

d) Tutor

D) BULLYING OTHERS

Have you ever bullied anyone? (please circle)   Yes   No

If you answered 'No' go on to section E.

▶

Bullying Questionnaire – continued

If you answered 'Yes'

i) What did you do?

....

....

ii) Why did you do it?

....

....

iii) Did you mean to hurt them? (please circle)   Yes   No

E) WITNESSING BULLYING

Have you ever seen anyone being bullied? (please circle)   Yes   No

If you answered 'No' go on to Section F.

If you answered 'Yes' what did you do? (please tick)

a) Walked by   c) Told someone

b) Tried to help   d) Other

F) DEALING WITH BULLYING

What is your opinion of bullying?

....

....

How do you think the school should deal with bullying?

....

....

How can we prevent bullying?

....

....

Why do you think bullies bully?

....

....

Thanks very much for taking the time to complete our questionnaire

Surveys are not the only form of gathering data about bullying. Interviews, focus groups, and sociograms are amongst the processes that can provide useful information about the experiences and concerns of pupils. Whatever form data-gathering takes, it needs to be planned and good practice shared with colleagues.

ACTIVITY

Planning to gather data on bullying

Participants: Staff

Time: 40–50 minutes

Equipment: Pen and paper and copies of **Planning to gather data on bullying** (see below).

In small groups first, before returning to the larger group, consider your responses to the questions raised. Make a time line that sets out the key dates when the data-gathering will happen.

Planning to gather data on bullying	
1 Focus	What do we want to find out?
	Will it just be about bullying or a broader range of experiences?
	Will we want information from everyone or just those who bully or are bullied?
	What will be the main foci, e.g. definition, experiences, observation, knowledge?
2 Method	What is the best way to achieve what we want?
	Who will we gather information from?
	What ethical problems do we have to consider, e.g. confidentiality?
	Who will be made aware of our findings?
3 Administration	Who will be involved and to what level?
	How many people will we collect information from?
	When will we collect the data?
4 Analysis	How will we analyse the data?
	Who will analyse it?
5 Outcome	What will we do with the data?
	Will we publish the results?
6 Review	How and when will we review the data-gathering process?

Secondary schools keen to recruit, often in competitive environments, make extensive arrangements to monitor pupils in the process of transition at Year 7 and, where they have communicated with primary schools, ensure that, when they become aware of a bullying relationship, those pupils are separated. Such is the success of these and other transition arrangements that pupils often report low levels of bullying and that one of their greatest fears of the 'big school' has not occurred. Years 8 and 9 present a different story and reported levels usually rise during this time (Lee, 1993) which may be connected to a relaxation in the monitoring and management process or the establishment of new relationships. However, such simplistic criteria as the number of reported incidents fails to acknowledge that creating cultures or developing systems in which it is safe to tell can have the effect of causing incidence levels to rise; indeed, *increased reported levels may be a symptom of success rather than of failure*. If prevention of bullying is known to begin and end with a regime predicated on punishment and fear then it is less likely that those who are bullied, those who watch and those who know will come forward. On the other hand, if it is based upon clarity and consistency of action, and a variety of preventative approaches that seek to nurture positive relationships through openness, then pupils may feel that it is safe to come forward. Surveys are not just about gathering information, they are a way of rendering pupils' experiences transparent

Playground/Meal-Time Assistants (MTAs)

Bullying is often associated with the playground and, consequently, anti-bullying strategies have included developing safe well-maintained playgrounds on which all pupils have the right to feel safe and enjoy their leisure time. Blatchford (1998) underlines the importance of playground design, the need for training supervisory staff and their role in nurturing positive interpersonal relationships in anti-bullying initiatives. Many groups, including parents and pupils, can become involved in playground design. Boulton (1995) views the playground as significant and notes that victims tend to be engaged in significantly fewer rule-based games, adding that social skills training for victims of bullying based on gaining entry in such rule-based games decreases the likelihood of them being vulnerable to the bullies.

The playground is a place of two contrasting images. In one it can be a positive part of school life where children have fun and learn to socialize and, in the other, it can be perceived as a centre of aggression and characterized by many pupils being unhappy at the expense of the pleasure of a few. Certainly it offers an arena in which older or more powerful pupils can exert a negative influence over others. However, it would be myopic and simplistic to see bullying as a playground matter only. Children decide to pick on their peers, and bullying relationships become established in various places and at various times, including when the pupils are in the classroom, and the decision to bully and the selection of the victim often takes place elsewhere. Nonetheless, certain factors will influence levels of bullying, such as supervision and the playground environment itself. We need to examine the environment and, when considering improvements, it may be possible to ask the children to contribute to the design and function of the playground as part of learning to use their power in a constructive way. Whilst it correct to say that some playgrounds get the playground bullying that the environment deserves, it has to be recognized that creating beautiful play environments may well be both expensive and time-consuming. One subject that will always attract debate is the use of the playground for football, especially as it often involves only boys, yet many playgrounds are of little use for anything else.

Meal-time assistants are in the front line of anti-bullying campaigns in the playground and are often caught in the middle of the bullying problem and, accepting that bullying is a relationship issue, they need to understand and be informed of the relationships between the children in their care. They are a group of people who often possess low professional esteem and earn low wages, yet they also possess power and opportunity to bring positive change. The Elton Report (DES, 1989) acknowledged that lunchtime supervisors are both vital and neglected, and that there was a need for them to be trained in behaviour management. Such training has been a piecemeal process and has lacked coherence, which is surprising given that teachers often report that the worst part of the day, in terms of pupil behaviour, is after lunch. There are three main problems:

1 *Communication*. This can be enhanced if MTAs are given information about school matters or pupils experiencing difficulties but this takes that rare commodity – time. All too often their sole focus is the dining hall, the queue to get into it and the playground. There are simple ways of improving communication such as:

   (a) information bulletins in which MTAs are included;

   (b) their own noticeboards;

   (c) communication books;

   (d) regular chances to meet with staff (not always the headteacher);

   (e) ensuring that they receive copies of relevant policies, even better if they are part of the creation of them;

   (f) ensuring that they are greeted and/or gathered together to report matters after their duty is completed;

   (g) establishing an efficient system that deals with the absence of an MTA;

   (h) assigning MTAs to classes for a short time before or after lunch so that they begin to develop relationships and gain knowledge about concerns over particular pupils.

2 *Lack of status or confusion over role.* It is essential that there are agreed roles and responsibilities. Meal-time assistants often find themselves contradicted, ignored and receiving mixed messages – are they 'members of staff'? If so, why do they not go to staff meetings? Confusion develops over their authority; for example, who is in charge when pupils are eating with teachers or when children are allowed in the classroom during lunchtimes? Certainly where there are meetings about behaviour they should attend and omission could be construed as a 'put down'. They need to feel valued and supported, and much can be done to improve their status, such as inviting them to attend key assemblies and other events.

3 *Lack of training.* They need more than first-aid training, and should know what help sick children need, certain child protection issues and especially the anti-bullying policy. Like other staff they would benefit from working on defining bullying because it develops consensus and involves them in the process.

A valuable addition to training might include rehearsing opening sentences for intervention, e.g. calmly stating: 'What is happening here? Dean looks very unhappy', when the victim is too frightened to admit involvement; or 'I'm sorry to interrupt but I need Jenny to take a message for me', if there is a perceived need to gain more information or probe whether the game that is being played is safe yet avoid being blaming or judgemental.

Meal-time assistants can also work with other staff to find the key areas of the playground where bullying takes place and they can work together on avoiding labelling children being involved in problem behaviour and not being problem children. Below is a checklist that aims to provide a starting point for approaches to avoiding 'fanning the flames' of aggression. It is neither complete nor comprehensive but it serves to begin discussions and provide suggestions.

MTA Checklist

1 Always try to keep calm, polite.

2 Encourage pupils and praise them.

3 Value the friendship of any child.

4 Listen well.

5 Label the behaviour, not the child.

6 Be careful not transmit a message of panic by rushing to a bullying scene.

7 Try not to jump to conclusions.

8 Avoid being sidetracked.

9 Avoid sarcasm and putdowns.

10 Avoid threats – especially if they will not or cannot be carried out.

11 Avoid using teachers as controls as this undermines your personal authority.

12 Set up a 'time out' system.

13 Consider 'tracking' or 'shadowing' pupils who are of concern.

14 If sanctions are used, make sure that there is a hierarchy of them, thereby avoiding using the most powerful weapon first.

15 If the pupils tell you there are '*hot spots*,' places where bullying often takes place (so often toilets!), then convene a group with staff to decide how best to monitor those spots.

16 Catch pupils being good and tell them. Pass on information especially about good behaviour and let the children know it is passed on and valued.

17 Join in a co-ordinated review of the playground and the games that children play.

18 Try for 'win-win' solutions as assertiveness techniques are important.

19 Use yellow card and red card systems. Whatever the reward or sanction system, ensure that they are agreed with teaching staff and in sympathy with what is happening elsewhere in the school.

20 Improve the quality of wet playtimes, especially the notion of 'theme' rooms, as it helps to break up the dynamics of the classroom relationships in which bullying may exist.

21 It is completely acceptable to ask for help when you need it and it is certainly not an admission of failure.

Meal-time assistants are subject to criticism and, thankfully, celebration from a variety of quarters. There also follow representative comments (below) from a selection of parents and pupils in a primary school which have implications for the training, status and communication, and which have been incorporated into an activity.

ACTIVITY

Enhancing the role of meal-time assistants

Participants: Staff

Time: 40 minutes

Equipment: Copies of **Pupils and parents on the effectiveness of MTAs** (see below) will need to be photocopied and distributed to groups.

In the smaller groups address the following questions:

1 How valid are the comments in relation to MTAs at your school?

2 What changes would you like to make that would deal with perceived problems?

3 What are the implications for training and resourcing?

Copies of the advice sheet (MTA Checklist, page 70) are now distributed and in groups staff consider how many of the items are relevant and which ones will form part of the policy. The larger group is reconvened and ideas shared before considering, 'What are the implications for professional development for MTAs'?

Pupils and parents on the effectiveness of MTAs

Parents	Some MTAs are of the opinion that discipline is nothing to do with them. I think they tend to ignore it, unless it gets physical, and don't intervene enough. I am sure most MTAs miss half of what occurs at playtimes as the job of overseeing those amounts of people all at once would be quite daunting. They have no real authoritative role. Some dinner ladies have the patience to listen and try and sort out problems and some don't. I feel that the role of the MTAs is not to get involved with dealing with such problems. However, they are important as observers and should liaise with teachers.
Pupils	Sometimes when I ask a dinner lady they sometimes don't listen. They just walk around blind as bats. Someone's had a fight right in front of Miss X before and she didn't notice. They don't really do anything. Whenever I get hurt the dinner ladies don't care a bit and that really worries me. All they say is don't go near them or say to the person who bullied don't do it again. They could listen to you and take more notice and sort out the problems. All they do is stay away from her or him and it doesn't work. Put more of them where bullying take place.

Managing Bullying Actions and Bullying Relationships

However determined policy-makers are to create an environment in which to bully would be anathema, bullying will still take place, and it is then that clear strategies of post-event management need to be in place and they need to be made known to all parties *as part of a clear preventative strategy*. Like all the ideas raised on the subject of awareness-raising the key issues will be contextual – what kind of school are we and what kind of culture do we want to become?

Approaches to post-event management can be broadly divided into two, based on whether adults or children play the key roles in dealing with the bullying. There is a further dimension to adult intervention and that is whether it is characterized by adults using their power and authority either to impose sanctions and solutions or using more counselling-based techniques. Similarly, pupil involvement can be part of a sanction-based approach or one that seeks a form of reconciliation and is limited by the control that pupils have been permitted to, or can legitimately, assume. If the premise that bullying is a phenomenon which is embedded in pupil culture is accurate, then placing pupils at the centre of proposed solutions has merits. Ultimately, the decision to pass responsibility to pupils is made by adults, and whether pupils play a leading role is dependent on adults initiating or licensing it does not alter the fact that responsibility for resolving bullying in school rests with teachers and other adults, especially the headteacher and the governing body. What follows is a consideration of the main strategies to be employed.

Working with the Bully

Bullies usually represent the major challenge to those staff dealing with bullying as their behaviour arouses outrage, fuelled by parents of victims demanding retribution and punitive approaches. The emotions that bullies arouse are understandable and the desire to respond to such emotions equally understandable. However, it is important to consider whether any intervention leads to a change in behaviour or merely makes sure that pupils are more careful and do not get caught in the future. Central to how bullying is dealt with are how staff feel about punishment and the potential of sanctions to bring about change, and it is important to consider what is meant by justice and what forms this can take.

Accepting the idea that there is more than one form of bully, it would seem logical that there is also more than one way of dealing with bullies. Rigby (1996) talks of three approaches. First, there is the *legalistic* approach which, as the name suggests, invokes very clear action that will be taken immediately all the necessary information has been found. This sends a clear message of non-tolerance but seeking the truth is very time-consuming and this approach is unlikely to lead to reconciliation. Second, the *moralistic* approach, focuses on compliance based on an acknowledgement that it is wrong to bully and appeals to a moral 'rightness' but there may be no engagement with the values of the bully. Finally, there is the *humanistic* approach where there is regard for the bully as a person but not for their behaviour, and attempts to change the behaviour of the bully are made through counselling. This can be seen as a 'soft option', especially by parents.

It may be that a school considers all three categories as a basis for decision-making on how they handle bullies. For example, one of the criteria for the choice could be whether the bullying was the first reported incident or whether the perpetrator has been involved in many incidents, i.e. whether it is a 'bullying action' or 'bullying relationship'. All the above focus on the bully and indicate that responsibility for resolution rests solely with them, which may be a narrow and ultimately fruitless approach.

Punishing the Bully

The least interventionist method that staff can deploy is being a role model. By being directive, clear and firm, but never cruel or aggressive, staff provide an exemplar for their pupils to emulate. In employing their own authority, adults call upon their own size, authority, age or status, although these factors diminish somewhat with older pupils! Bullies have the capacity to generate anger, especially from parents of the victims who are rightly outraged, and this anger can fuel a desire to punish. Whatever the anger felt by staff, if it is conveyed to perpetrators then it is likely that it will foster resentment in the bully, ensure that they have learned that aggression pays off and the victim will suffer again, and they will make sure they do not get caught in the future. Yet away from the emotional storm that bullying generates anger is evident. Consider these two statements 'show the bullies how disgusting they are' and 'punish bullies … show him what you are putting on file and make him pay for whatever time it cost you to sort out'. These are two uncited quotations from the literature on bullying and they convey not only an understandable outrage, but also an anger that is directed at a person and not their behaviour – it is *bullying* that is 'disgusting' not the *bully*. Depending on definitions of bullying and school contexts, a high proportion of the school population, staff included, might be thought to be 'disgusting' if we follow this line of argument.

The focus here is principally on dealing with perpetrators, with a perceived need to employ corrective techniques and, perhaps to punish. Inherent within this are the dangers of action becoming bullying itself, especially if hurt is defined by the recipient. An alternative way of looking at this is that the authority of the teacher comes to compensate for any lack of power possessed by victims and it provides a balance of power. Elliott's (1997a) mentions punishment, but not 'aggressive' punishment, with the emphasis placed on making amends and apologizing publicly or privately, and here there are links with restorative justice. The public element is one that needs to be considered carefully as to apologize in public may have the effect of ensuring that such humiliation is something that pupil will not want to experience again and they will never bully again or, at least, never be caught. Alternatively publicly apologizing can have the effect of institutionalizing the perpetrator's role as a bully and reinforcing his or her status as a power to be feared.

There are advocates of a strident application of authoritarian strategies in recommending that teachers punish bullies and certainly, at a time when emotions run high and there is pressure being brought to bear by parents, it is understandable. The long-term impact, with damage to sometimes vulnerable self-esteem, needs careful consideration and punitive treatments could have a negative effect, reinforcing a view that being in possession of power invites opportunities to bully. What is needed is balanced, thought-through consensus of the value of sanction based approaches and the kinds that might work in the context of the school.

We have already seen that a simple category, 'bully', is a simplification and this has management implications. 'Passive bullies', those who form part of groups that bully, have been said to do so because of a need for self-protection. Techniques employed with this group look to arouse sympathy, understanding, even remorse, and each member of the group assumes responsibility for what has happened.

ACTIVITY

The drawbacks of punishing bullies

Participants: Staff

Time: 50 minutes

Equipment: Photocopies of **The drawbacks of punishing bullies** (see below) and, perhaps, **Retributive justice versus restorative justice** (pages 75–6) will be required.

In small groups discuss and complete **The drawbacks of punishing bullies** and ways in which it might be used.

1 Discuss in groups of three and decide whether the group 'totally agree'(A) with the statement, 'partly agree'(P) or 'totally disagree' (D).

2 Discuss findings in the larger group and consider where there is consensus and disagreement.

Reconvene the larger group and consider what statements you could make in an anti-bullying policy document that represents agreement on sanctions.

The drawbacks of punishing bullies

The drawbacks of punishing bullies are that it:	A, P or D
Can foster anxiety and resentment	
Is often short-lived and has only an initial effect	
Encourages pupils to develop strategies for not getting caught in the future	
Does not promote good behaviour	
May be an inappropriate model for human relationships	
Does not deal with the cause of the bullying or alter a bullying relationship	
Publicizes the bullying — everyone gets to know	
But when used it should be:	
Timed properly, used sparingly	
An expression of disapproval given in the interests of the class or school	

▶

The drawbacks of punishing bullies continued	
But when used it should be:	
Appropriate for the misdemeanour	
Accepted as just	
Related to anti-bullying policy	
Be unpleasant — some children like to be sent into the warm classroom on a cold day	
Not a punishment for staff (keeping pupils in and not getting a break yourself!)	

Restorative Justice and Bullying

In recent years there have been changes amongst those dealing with youth crime in particular, and a number of theories have evolved. One example is *conferencing* which is a meeting of families of both victims and offenders and the *reintegrative shaming process* (Braithwaite, 1989) in which offenders have their behaviour disapproved of by those close to them, but who also provide support in the reintegration process. Broadly speaking such processes aim at bringing change in behaviour without a focus on denial of liberty. Zehr (1990) compared traditional retributive justice philosophy with restorative justice values and ideas and I have applied his model to the management of bullying in school.

Retributive justice versus restorative justice	
Retributive justice	**Restorative justice**
Bullying is breaking the school rules and running counter to school policy.	Bullying is a behaviour that adversely affects others.
Attention to rules and procedures.	Attention to relationships and positive outcomes.
Focuses on the past — what happened?	Focuses on the present and the future — what will happen?
Focus on establishing blame or guilt — who bullied?	Focus on expressing feelings and needs.
Imposition of painful or unpleasant punishment as a deterrent and treatment.	Restitution as a means of restoring all parties. Reconciliation and responsibility for the future.
Bully accountable through receiving punishment.	Bully accountable through understanding the hurt caused, seeing it as a consequence of a choice and helping to put things right.

▶

75

Retributive justice versus restorative justice – continued	
Adversarial relationship: bully is in conflict with person in authority who determines punishment.	Dialogue and negotiation – all parties involved in communicating and co-operating with each other.
Bullying represented as impersonal: the individual versus school.	Bullying recognized as interpersonal conflict from which learning emerges.
One social injury, i.e. bullying may be replaced by another.	Focus on repair of social injury or damage.
School community are spectators, represented by member of staff dealing with the situation.	School community involved in facilitating restoration.
People affected by bullying not necessarily involved. Victim's needs ignored adding to powerlessness.	Encouragement of all concerned to be involved, including bystanders.

Restorative justice aims to bring about the long-term change in relationships, based upon the idea that bullies will meet the people who have been affected by their behaviour, together with trained mediators. Many, but not all, victims of criminal behaviour have attested to the value of the process and how it has helped them to put the trauma behind them. The starting point for a school focus is becoming involved in mediation and conferencing which creates opportunities for active listening, recognition of the situation of others, empowerment, perhaps apology and maybe forgiveness. However, for emotional healing to take place, the wider community has a role to play in supporting both victims and offenders to move on after the mediation process. What cannot happen is that all that has been achieved becomes undermined by thoughtless responses from pupils and staff and, for this reason alone, it is important that any process that demands changes in relationships takes place in an environment in which the whole school is aware and, even better, skilled.

A teacher who understands and practises a restorative approach recognizes that basis needs, not just surface behaviours, need addressing. These include low self-esteem, a lack of communication skills and poor co-operation, which contrasts with the desired classroom which is full of pupils and adults with high self-esteem, who communicate effectively and who enjoy working together. There are many arenas in which these key attributes can be developed and circle time, especially for younger pupils, is a starting point in developing an environment conducive to problem-solving, mediation and expressing emotions. Failure to understand emotions leaves resentment and the conflict is likely to erupt again.

The School Council

There is growing contemporary interest in the development of pupil involvement in decision-making in schools. The concept of a *school council* is one that is attracting a lot of interest because children gain:

- increased understanding of their problems;

- increased confidence and self-esteem and the skills required to speak out;

- a say in matters that concern them;

- opportunities for social and moral development;

- greater understanding of the school;

- a genuine chance to make a difference;

- an opportunity to learn about how organizations function;

- a chance to share problems and derive solutions for them;

In return the school gets:

- increased awareness of the key issues for pupils;

- pupils' assistance in policy development;

- using pupils' energy to contribute positively;

- increased consensus for school policies;

- consultation process;

- increased pupils' sense of ownership of the school including the grounds.

Developing a school council is not a simple matter with the central problems being how much real power are staff prepared to give to the council and what will be the influence of their deliberations on the management of the school. Having decided the parameters, a number of other matters follow, e.g. gender balance, age representation, duration of service, reliability, ability and sense of responsibility of students, training needs; involvement of adults (not just teachers), regularity of meetings, whether it should have a budget and be monitored.

An important decision is whether there should be a link teacher to provide the role of mentor, act as a reference point for other staff and deal with procedural matters such as the next meeting. The status given to such a member of staff will give a clear message about the importance the school council.

The No Blame Approach and the Shared Concern Method

Pikas's 'shared concern method' and the similar 'no blame approach' of Robinson and Maines are amongst the most distinctive approaches to post-event intervention to be deployed in schools, and they have much in common. Both methods demand that teachers or other adults spend time working with the victimized, the bullies and those who were nearby or were aware of what happened. They perceive perpetrators and those who are bystanders as a group that will be encouraged to share responsibility through a series of meetings. The adult orientates the group towards the future and to solving the problem of bullying without there being a need for punishment for previous actions. Emphasis is not on the past but towards a relationship that has a positive future and whether differences can be resolved. Of all the theoretical stances behind 'no blame' is the urge, indicated in the title, to abandon blaming bullies. Given the emotions and pressures that discovery of bullying can bring, particularly from parents, not to punish but to work positively with bullies is challenging.

Schools thinking of exploring the value of either form of approach will need to read a more comprehensive version of the stages and think about the implications for the whole school. Like any structured approach they place demands on time and skill but their existence in schools conveys a message that the school takes bullying seriously and is prepared to involve a variety of parties in order to bring about resolution.

The approaches can be summarized in the following steps.

The shared concern method and the no blame approach		
Step	No blame approach: action	Shared concern method: action
1	Interview with the victim	Meet with the involved individually
2	Meet with the involved	Interview with the victim
3	Explain the problem	Establish if they contribute to problem
4	Share responsibility	Meet with involved in a group
5	Ask the group for ideas	Establish the shared concern for the victim
6	Leave it up to them	Hold resolution meeting with all involved
7	Meet them again	Meet them again

Both methods have as a basis perceiving the perpetrator and those who are bystanders as a group and a clear emphasis upon shared responsibility generated through a series of meetings. The teacher functions in the role of data gatherer, active listener and aims to orientate the group towards the future. To that end, there is minimal discussion of what happened or why it happened. Facilitators work with groups in order to draw upon the group's potential to change towards more positive interactions with the victim and the assumption that the onus to stop the bullying rests with them not the victim.

However, there are key differences:

■ The 'shared concern method' is highly structured and scripted and, whilst the 'no blame approach' has very clear stages, the guidance given permits a more flexible approach.

■ In the 'shared concern method', bullies are interviewed singly and before any meeting with a victim. With the 'no blame approach', the feelings of the victim are ascertained before a group meeting of the bullies and any pupils who were involved or nearby.

- In the 'no blame approach', much is made of the feelings of victims and the transmission of the record of those feelings to perpetrators. With 'shared concern' the focus is on the action.

- Pikas commends his approach for pupils over the age of 9 and in the case of group bullying, often called 'mobbing' in his native Scandinavia. Maines and Robinson suggest that their approach is also suitable for 'one-to-one' bullying.

Maines and Robinson (1992) disapprove of the need for full investigation into what pupils say happened on the basis that teachers and other adults often receive the answers that the pupil think those adults want to hear. Not only does the search for the truth lead to little more than perspectives of what transpired, but it becomes an invitation for perpetrators to offer a contradictory account in seeking to extract themselves from blame. The 'no blame approach' has been embellished with advice that bullying should not be regarded as 'abnormal or evil' (Maines and Robinson, 1991) as many pupils collude with bullying. The mobilization of pupils who are aware of what is happening is central to both forms of post-event management, although it raises the question of whether there are boundaries around awareness and who is alert to what is happening. Blaming bullies and bystanders may be productive and, in the modern busy school, where time has become a rare commodity, the search for accurate accounts of incidents would seem counter-productive. Using that time to bring about reconciliation between pupils may have advantages over seeking the origins of conflict and precisely attributing blame.

One of the fundamental issues raised by support-based techniques is rejection of advice that urges change in the victim. This is because it locates responsibility with victims and implies it is their fault. If they were to change then all would be well. What initially drew the attention of other pupils and led to the victimization may well be capable of change, although it is unlikely, but once the bullying relationship becomes established it is not dependent on the original characteristic which triggered that attention. Another reason for not requiring change from victims is that they are highly likely to feel inadequate as a result of the bullying, therefore to urge a change in their behaviour further dents their fragile self esteem.

The need to change behaviour rests with perpetrators and bystanders in most cases. However, there is no single method that provides the simple answer to the complex issue that is bullying in schools. For example, on the subject of change in victims, what should we do about the provocative victim, the pupil who 'calls forth' the bullying and invites others to pick on them? Jake, a 15-year-old secondary age pupil that I worked with, experienced taunting and bullying in school and out of it. His parents were considering withdrawing him from the school and there were growing frustrations being experienced by Jake, his parents and the staff. When we talked about his experiences, he expressed outrage that he should be picked on for his appearance. At school he was less distinctive and had a compliant, if liberal, interpretation of the school uniform. Outside school he often wore make-up and occasionally a skirt. It was simply a fashion statement he stated and underlined his right to dress as he wanted (a right endorsed by his parents). He stated that he felt that his form of dress determined why he was being picked on, but it was an expression of his individuality. The central questions here are:

- Do we celebrate individuality even when the expression of it clearly leads to difficulties?

- Whose behaviour needs to change in cases like this?

ACTIVITY

The no blame approach and the shared concern method

Participants: Staff

Time: 40 minutes

Equipment: Photocopies of table **The no blame approach and the shared concern method** (page 78)
                are required.

In groups discuss the two approaches described above and consider the following questions:

1   What are the group's feelings about these non-punitive approaches?

2   What age of pupils would benefit from them?

3   What adaptations, if any, might need to be made for younger pupils?

4   What are the implications of 'no blame' and 'shared concern' for working with parents?

5   What are the group's feelings about not requiring change in the victim's appearance or behaviour?

6   Is the outcome likely to be a genuine attempt to resolve the conflict or a feeling amongst perpetrators that
    they 'got away with it'?

Meet in the larger group and, if there is an endorsement of one approach, consider:

1   How and when will it be introduced?

2   What are the implications for professional development?

Both techniques have been employed in schools and case studies of their application indicate merit in them, although there is a need for independent evaluations. However, difficulties in evaluating their success or otherwise may render any evidence of their worth problematic. It is just as likely that the presence of a clear, consistent approach, rather than the nature of that approach, may influence improvements in incidence levels of bullying. In any case, as stated before, incidence levels alone appear a dubious barometer of success or failure.

Certainly there remain unanswered questions about both interventions. For example, repair to relationships may be one facet of the matter, but the damage to property and repayment of extorted money are not addressed by such approaches. Nonetheless, the encouragement of disclosure, the countering of secrecy and the knowledge that positive action has been taken without an overtly punitive component being employed has much to commend it.

Assertiveness Training

There are two ways in which assertiveness can be employed as a preventa/tive technique. First, there is assertiveness training for all which has the value of assisting *all pupils*, giving perpetrators alternative ways of acting, victims the capacity to withstand bullying and respond without aggression and bystanders the opportunity to develop ways of intervening non-aggressively in support of victims. Moving in this direction might lead to the development of assertiveness training for all, including teaching staff, teaching assistants, secretarial staff and meal-time assistants. Second, there is a focus on assertiveness training for those *who have been victims* or are potential victims with the ambition of helping them to become members of the non-bullied group, through the development of skills for coping effectively with the bullying. This demands change from those pupils who are 'picked on'. Herein is a dilemma for staff as, touched on previously, it could be argued that children have the right to be the way they are, they should not be bullied and the onus to change should be on perpetrators. However, changing the attitude and behaviour of bullies may be more difficult than teaching victims strategies, because perpetrators often have their behaviour rendered legitimate by parents who bully and by teachers who have allowed the bullying to go on uninterrupted.

The theoretical basis of assertiveness is the notion that individuals possess basic human rights including to:

- be treated with respect;

- be listened to and taken seriously;

- make mistakes and be responsible for them;

- say 'no' without feeling guilty;

- ask for what you want and acknowledge the other party's right to say 'no';

- ask for information;

- say 'I do not understand'.

At the heart of assertiveness training is recognition that pupils are faced with four ways of behaving and having needs met and that there are also ways of responding to being bullied and that aggression is not a positive response. The four ways are:

Direct aggression	Indirect aggression
My rights are more important than yours.	Your rights are not important to me, although I may lead you to believe that they are.
Passive aggression	Assertiveness
Your rights are more important than mine.	Our rights are of equal importance.

Central to the thinking behind being assertive is the idea of equality of rights, and therefore it helps to restore imbalances in power that have developed in a relationship. Assertive responses often include 'I' statements, and are accompanied by exuding confidence and by a body language that matches the message being conveyed. What is said and the way that it is said are significant parts of the message, but body language is a highly, maybe the most, significant part of any communication. Pupils need to rehearse and role-play their responses as part of their assertiveness training.

Mick tells Chris that, if he doesn't do everything that he says, he will tell the teacher that Chris was being naughty. Chris replies …	
Direct aggression	Don't you dare threaten me. If you tell the teacher I will beat you up.
Indirect aggression	That will be clever of you. Are you sure you can remember who the teacher is?
Passive aggression	Er, um, well okay. I guess I will have to do what you say.
Assertiveness	I am not intending to do what you say and your threats will not make me do anything.

Every time Jenny passes Adele she pulls her long hair. She knows that it hurts her.	
Direct aggression	Oi, you, cut it out or I will pull your hair.
Indirect aggression	Why are you pulling my hair – is it the only way you can get attention at playtime?
Passive aggression	Don't do it, it hurts me and if you carry on you will make me upset.
Assertiveness	I don't like what you are doing and I want you to stop it now.

The above illustrations are examples of direct, face-to-face bullying but the less direct forms such as spitting in someone's drink and saying that they will be forced to drink it or calling names out of earshot, are unlikely to be countered by assertiveness approaches which are based on direct communication with perpetrators. Bullies employ direct aggression if the form of the bullying is physical and will resort to less direct forms if there is a desire to socially isolate.

Being assertive, like many ideas explored in this book, demands pupils learning about them, what they mean and how to carry them out in practice. Not everyone can become assertive overnight and then they may not be assertive in all contexts. Someone can be assertive on a playground but much more passive at home. Nonetheless, results from the Sheffield Project, noted increased self-esteem and self-confidence in pupils who participated in assertiveness training (DfE, 1994). These included:

- how to be positive, yet avoid boasting;

- friendship maintenance;

- being aware of their own feelings and emotions and those of others;

- positive body language and relaxation training.

Solution-Focused Brief Therapy

All the methods mentioned in this chapter demand training, preparation and setting in the culture of the school. Brief therapy is no exception but it is unique in this context in that it should be undertaken by a counselling practitioner familiar with it. It has been included because:

■ some schools have just such a person working with them;

■ it provides a contrast to more punitive notions;

■ it is not based upon searching for what happened, but helps the victim to look to the future without being disempowered by supporting adults.

Instead of focusing on the problem, brief therapy seeks solutions and invites victims to 'reframe' their experiences to provide solutions. It places less emphasis on examining past failures and looks to find past successes – when were things good? Less time is spent explaining problems, pinpointing weaknesses and failings, and more time is spent on explaining progress, pinpointing strengths and resources. It focuses less on blaming people perceived as responsible for bullying and focuses more on acknowledging people who have contributed to the solution. Its future orientation and optimism are summarized by:

Imagine that after you have gone to bed tonight, while you are sleeping a miracle happens and the problems that brought you here today are resolved. When you wake up in the morning, how will you know the miracle has happened?

The following table outlines the main steps.

The stages of brief therapy in a bullying context

Stage	Key questions or comments
1 Other people's perspectives How others would recognize change.	How will other family members know about progress in resolving the bullying? How will friends know that the bullying has stopped? What will they see you doing that is different? How will your friends tell that you have reached your target?
2 Exception finding When things were better or handled well.	When was the last time that it did not happen? When did you feel safer? Which pupils offered support? Which adults dealt effectively with bullies?
3 Scaling Attempts are made to quantify the problem.	On a scale of 1 to 10, with 1 being the worst things have been and 10 representing how you want things to be, where are you now? What tells you have moved from 1 to 3 or 7 to 8? What would be a reasonable position to aim for now?
4 Locating resources An appraisal is made of skills and strengths and who was helpful.	How has the pupil dealt with the bullying in the past? What personal strengths can be identified from this? Who were the effective people that they draw upon for support?

The stages of brief therapy in a bullying context – continued	
5 Coping How pupils are coping and what or who is supportive.	How do you deal with it? Who helps you? What approaches have appeared to work? When are things okay?
6 Stop things getting worse The need for additional support to provide an initial coping device.	Who would you be happy to have to help us? Who can help us provide support and with whom you would feel safe?
7 Constructive feedback It is important to keep students in touch with what they are doing well, how their own attitude is helping, evidence of determination, perseverance or creative thinking	You have been good at … You have helped me by being … You have kept going very well. That was a great idea and it has worked well.
8 Ending Reminds pupils of indicators of progress and refers to goals stated at start of session.	We agreed that we need to look out for … We started by saying that … We decided that things would be improving if …

Brief therapy seeks to help pupils who are bullied to 'reframe' their situation and to learn to deal with bullying by visualizing it differently and reacting in ways that are assertive, not aggressive. They are supported in developing techniques that help overcome the torment of the bully and which show bystanders that they are capable of withstanding attempts to disempower them. Lines (2002) cautions against using this approach with provocative victims as they lack the social skills and imagination required to benefit from the technique.

Involving and Empowering Pupils

A comprehensive collection of data on how children respond to bullying experiences is La Fontaine's (1991) analysis of 'Childline' telephone calls over a period of three months. Amongst the findings of all the data gathered anonymously was that:

- reporting it, in itself, did not always resolve matters;

- children were prepared to speak out against bullying;

- children wanted to be involved in dealing with bullying.

Peer involvement in prevention and response to bullying forms a natural part of a school in which children are invited to contribute to decisions at a variety of levels including teaching and learning issues and policy formulation. As well as possibly witnessing bullying and knowing the participants, supposedly non-involved pupils are essential to creating the social context that negates or nurtures it. As stated before, ultimate responsibility for developing, permitting and supporting interventions and addressing the bullying itself rests with staff, i.e. pupils can only become active participants if they are allowed to do so, and what follows are techniques or methods that involve students but are reliant on adults for training, monitoring and, probably, their success or otherwise.

Bully Courts

Those who seek to resolve bullying issues look to the criminal court system and replicate elements of it, i.e. bully courts to create systems that deal with bullying but also seek to create a climate of fear that prevents bully. Regarding pupils being formally given increased authority in schools, long before the subject of school bullying became a more open one, there had been experimentation with pupils having the power to censure through 'courts'. One of the earliest examples is Laslett's (1982) consideration of a 'court', administered by pupils in a day special school aimed at giving them power over their peers. The concept has been adopted and advocated by others. In one middle school not only was a court set up, but also legalistic language used to structure procedures, i.e. bench, defendant and complainant. Initial punishments were reported as 'Draconian' (Brier and Ahmad, 1991) but more moderation prevailed as the court became established. Benefits were claimed through a statistical comparison with year groups in which no courts operated, which again raises the question: was it the *specific* intervention or simply that something was being done?

Endorsement of 'bully courts' has come from Elliott (1997b), who rightly urges that they should form part of a whole-school policy. She claims that they are an effective way of getting students involved in solving their own problems in a constructive manner and that is to be applauded. She also adds that a better name for these may be 'councils' or 'arbitration panels'. There are implications here in charging pupils to judge others who have been labelled 'bullies' for a 'crime' that raise complex issues in the selection of cases and, inevitably, definition. In addition to punishing potentially innocent pupils, the complexities of deciding *what the 'crime' of bullying is* places levels of responsibility on the shoulders of a group of pupils who do not formulate notions in the same way as adults. Other reservations about bully courts centre on teachers' apprehensions about their potential for unduly punitive 'sentences' and the opportunity that they represent to formalize the very behaviour that they were seeking to counter – bullying, the powerful having power to hurt the powerless. The prevailing stance seems to have been according bullies 'a touch of their own medicine'. A study of pupil courts in 30 London schools referred to punishments such as staying after school and being made to eat lunch in an isolated area (Ziegler and Rosenstein-Manner, 1991). In the case of the latter form of punishment it seems an anachronism to legitimize social isolation and replicating one of the behaviours that bullies themselves employ.

Further concerns include that bullies themselves become elected to the court, the potential for public trial to render the bully an anti-hero and that such a form of dealing with bullying has little application for younger children. Central to the caution is that rigid, punitive approaches offer little likelihood of changing pupil behaviour and risk rendering bullying more clandestine.

Peer Support

The potential of peers to influence anti-bullying practices by adopting a role similar to that of a counselling role or peer support has many forms. As stated previously, the power to instigate and manage the systems within which pupils have been afforded this authority rests with adults (Cowie and Sharp, 1992), plus the maintenance and channelling of enthusiasm that leads to success rests with staff. There are many forms of peer support, and consideration must be given to key factors that influence which form to employ. One factor is the age of the pupils. Cowie and Wallace (2000) suggest that befriending, circle time, circles of friends and co-operative group work can be used with young children, that peer mediation and peer tutoring should be employed with old junior age pupils and that counselling-based interventions are best left until secondary school. Rightly, they urge that schools adopt a flexible attitude and children in early years can be helped through the development of listening and communication skills and the nurturing of celebration of difference which knows no age barriers or boundaries. Other factors such as the type of school and the enthusiasm and skills of staff will determine which approach is best suited. How often a particularly enthusiastic member of staff sets up and becomes the 'change driver' for a specific innovation, only to move on to another school and that innovation and its positive outcomes are left to wither and die. Whatever method is adopted, the quicker it becomes embedded and integrated into the culture of the school, and understood and championed by many staff and pupils, the better.

Befriending

As with all the peer support techniques befriending does not have to be seen as solely a means of dealing with bullying; it can also be used to help pupils who have experienced trauma or loss. It could help new pupils, pupils known to be experiencing emotional or social difficulties or who do not find making friends easy. Befriending encourages children to make deliberate attempts to become the friend of a classmate who is experiencing difficulties or who might be entering a situation that could be difficult. It is common practice in some schools to have a system of befriending new pupils, Year 11 work with Year 7 pupils and Year 6 with Year 3, although it is important to consider whether there should be provision for all new pupils to a school. Another consideration is whether befrienders should be selected pupils working with specifically identified newcomers or whether the system should be more general, which, if so, leads to difficult decisions about involving pupils known to have bullied others. Whatever the spectrum of involvement, befrienders need to be trained in enhancing their listening skills, how best to support and at what stage or in what kinds of case they should seek advice from adults.

There are many positive outcomes for those who befriend others, such as their:

- self-esteem is enhanced by their confidence in dealing with their peers and the positive feedback that usually follows;

- awareness and understanding of social and emotional issues is developed;

- social skills are acquired;

- qualities of responsibility and leadership are nurtured.

Circle Time

Circle time has been embraced by many staff working in schools. It is a process that has enormous potential if well structured, thought through and, like many of the techniques mentioned in this chapter, supported by professional training and good practice. Circle time makes use of many of the skills and complements the values of non-punitive approaches with its emphasis on mutual respect, active listening, empathy, problem-solving and celebration of difference. When it is undertaken as a casual, occasional opportunity to discuss an issue or, even worse, as a means of using up time, then a vital opportunity for personal and social growth becomes devalued. To ensure its status the circle should meet regularly and often, at least once a week, and include activities designed to increase awareness of self and others, co-operation, trust and precious self-esteem. It is an opportunity to evaluate friendship problems and bullying in an open forum in which there are no bystanders.

Co-operative Group Work

It is difficult to separate this form of peer support from what goes on in a good classroom. Pupils are taught the skills of collaboration through structured activities including dealing with conflict. Pupils are helped to:

- work together in groups other than friendship groups;

- adopting roles in groups such as leader, problem-solver and recorder of decisions;

- care for each other and respect decisions of others in the group;

- work out and adhere to rules;

- share information;

- share tasks loads in order to meet group objectives;

- discuss differences of opinion and conflict, including bullying, and seek to find resolution.

Co-operative games, trust-building and role play are all vehicles that staff can use to cultivate a strong group bond, but many staff will already employ the ideas above as part of their professional practice. This approach demands that they consider their structure, sequence and purpose and see how they can help to build a co-operative community.

Peer Counselling

Bullying is said to be nurtured by the secrecy that results from pupils' reluctance to inform teachers if they are being bullied. Having peers as a part of a support system, or as an initial source of information, may be a preferred course of action for those who are bullied. Peer counselling aims to change pupils' responses to bullying, from condoning and being ambivalent about it to viewing it as unacceptable. In working with perpetrators pupils work on acknowledgement that their actions were unacceptable and they wish to make a commitment to change.

One of the merits of peer counselling is the 'de-escalation' of the situation as it often results in minimizing the impact of pupils feeling unfairly treated which is associated with adults who put pressure on pupils to change their behaviour.

Using the telephone to provide a counselling-based 'bully line' in which peers provided a service that sometimes amounts to little more than listening to problems. Following a period of training by a member of staff, pupils were licensed to offer their support and the lack of staff involvement led to pupils assuming a role for management of the system. The principal benefits were deemed to be enhancement of self-esteem of the counsellors, often former victims themselves, and the acquisition of important interpersonal skills (Sharp, Sellars and Cowie, 1994).

Other more specific counselling approaches have been adopted such as 're-evaluation counselling' (Cartwright, 1996). This was a case study in which a school counsellor trained a group of students in this form of counselling, encouraging outward expression of inner feelings, such as hurt and anger. The trained group then offered a confidential counselling service that was open to bullies and victims.

Peer Mediation

Giving pupils skills, responsibility and, subsequently, power to mediate in bully/victim problems has led to a number of initiatives in schools, especially in the form of the development of peer mediation schemes. Before a consideration of mediation, which tends to be adopted by schools that are highly motivated in the way that they deal with bullying, a word of caution. In passing certain power to pupils to deal with incidents of bullying, a tension can arise for some staff. Professional responsibility demands that teachers have a significant say and considerable responsibility in handling situations and knowing what is happening in the classroom and the school. Transmitting authority to pupils by giving them a mediation role can mean encouraging associated notions of confidentiality according to Knights (1998), which may run counter to the idea of teachers being responsible for pupils' well-being.

However, there are many advantages to mediation including that adults are often limited in the degree to which they can invade the world of children, therefore, through mediation they can invite them to be actively involved in the resolution of bullying problems and give them the appropriate skills. Mediation says much about the core values that staff hold dear and how they wish to empower pupils rather than impose solutions from above. It is all too easy to see it as being of value for older pupils, but the skills required in mediators are important skills that should not be ignored in early years settings. I have known young children and children in a special school benefit in confidence and self-esteem from mediation training.

In a school context the usual pattern is for a team of two mediators working to encourage problem-solving between the people who are regarded as being in disagreement rather than bullying. Pupils need a programme of training which equips them with specific skills for mediating disputes. Training in interpersonal skills is essential and brings the advantage that as pupils move further up the school they can build upon those skills. Younger pupils would be taught to practise speaking and listening, taking turns and remaining calm and controlled. The same principal of identifying and developing basic skills for young pupils applies to other preventative approaches mentioned elsewhere in this book. By using mediation skills throughout a school for all ages of pupil, peer mediation becomes a preventative approach, not only a way of managing conflict.

Included in the skills are:

- active listening;

- reflection on feelings;

- clarification of what has been heard;

- body language;

- types of questioning;

- effective problem-solving.

Role-playing is used to practise newly acquired skills, such as mediating to resolve playground disagreements or what appears to be a bullying incident. In summary, the process demands that mediators meet with disputants and control the situation by affirming that pupils in dispute will adhere to the ground rules, including:

- allowing others to speak without interrupting them;

- speaking about others with respect;

- talking about the problem without blame or accusation.

Each disputant tells their side of the story and expresses their feelings about what has happened. The mediators listen carefully, non-judgementally, not dwelling on the past and what cannot be changed more than is necessary. Disputants are asked what they would each like to happen and, finally, are involved in exploring what might actually be done. The whole orientation of the meeting is the future (see Solution-focused brief therapy, pp. 82–4).

Peer mediation, then, is about:

- how we define bullying, for if power is one of the key components in a definition, then teaching pupils to use power positively and seek solutions rather than fuel aggressive situations is constructive;

- the attitude of the school, including the supposed 'non-involved' who, by remaining non-involved, could be considered to be colluding with bullying;

- the core values that a school holds dear with emphasis on empowering pupils rather than provide quick-fix solutions from above;

- how adults in schools view pupils and their preparation for life in a democratic world.

In practical terms, consideration needs to be given to the broader school setting. If a primary school has a well-established mediation system, it is likely that the pupils involved will have social skills that are different from those of their peers in other neighbouring primary schools. When the time for transition to secondary education comes, receiving schools need to know about these pupils and whether they will continue to deploy the skills of mediators who are likely to be confident in handling difficult situations within their own age group.

A second practical consideration is that peer mediation is not just about mediators, it is about the whole school and any project will be demanding at first. Pupils will need to be trained in difficult processes and considerable effort, time and skill involving techniques such as role-play, observing adults and their fellow pupils will be required, but the rewards are likely to counterbalance the investment. Schools which adopt such approaches are likely to note increases in pupils' self-esteem and social skills and learning.

A further benefit of mediation is that it challenges the bully, victim and rescuer model. It is often the case that, if the victim did not feel disempowered after the attentions of the bully, they will do after the rescuer has exposed their supposed inadequacies. Mediation is forward-seeking, brings balance and calm to a dispute and is solution focused rather than problem centred. The two parties change their role from powerful bully and powerless victim to people in dispute.

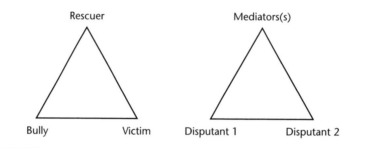

Merits of peer mediation include that it:

- provides children with vocabulary and interpersonal skills;

- can involve the whole school, including the 'non-involved', who by remaining so are colluding with bullying;

- leads to 'win-win' outcomes rather than 'win-lose';

- leads to fewer incidents and lower stress levels for all;

- prevents perpetrators feeling resentful and likely to continue to bully;

- prevents labeling of informants as 'dobbers', which becomes part of regimes of fear;

- provides perpetrators with a rare opportunity to develop empathy with others' feelings or responsibility for their actions;

- provides approaches at the bullying action stage, before it transforms into a bullying relationship.

Before considering setting up a programme, the following activity may help to reflect on key practices and principles.

ACTIVITY

Setting up a peer mediation project

Participants: Staff (considering setting a peer mediation pilot project)

Time: 40 minutes

Equipment: Photocopies of **Questions on peer mediation** (see below).

Staff discuss the 'questions' and agree an action plan for the introduction and monitoring of a pilot peer mediation programme in the school.

Questions on peer mediation

Issue	Question
Administration and management of the project	Are there advantages in support staff and/or pupils themselves being involved in the project management?
Whole school or just single group?	What will be the long-term impact as pupils move through the school or, more significantly, to other schools?
Pilot, duration	Should a 'pilot' group of mediators be trained? How long should the pilot programme be?
Training	Should the opportunity to train as mediators be given to those who are known to have bullied others or those who have been extensively picked on?
Parents informed/involved	What information will be passed on to parents? How can they be involved in the development of the scheme, if deemed desirable?
Monitoring	Who will undertake the monitoring? What form will it take?

What emerges from each peer support approach is that, although authority residing increasingly with pupils has been a common aspect, each has distinctive features and, therefore, evaluating their success, or otherwise, should embrace broad criteria including attitudinal change. Eslea and Smith (1998), in their questionnaire-based research into bullying in selected primary schools, found a significant increase in positive pupil attitudes to interventions in all four schools which had specific anti-bullying programmes, and this occurred irrespective of any changes in reported levels of bullying. It is not just about the behaviour but how people feel about it.

CHAPTER 6

How to Move your School Forward

Aside from the summary, this chapter suggests the top ten pieces of advice in a preventative strategy before concluding with one of the central themes of the book – that bullying reflects upon the school culture and can be part of it, but schools and the staff within them have the potential to make a significant difference. A comprehensive list of websites, organizations and resources comprises the final section.

Summing Up

In common with many people who write on and research into the multifaceted subject of bullying, I have occasionally mentioned incidence levels often measured by questionnaires. They are of value in that they provide data on 'before' and 'after' levels in appraising the efficacy or otherwise of specific intervention techniques and they demonstrate that bullying is, or is not, a widespread problem. Like many measures employed in measuring educational phenomena they evaluate the apparent extent of a problem or progress in quantitative terms, but reveal little about the context of the school, the feelings of stakeholders, the impact of a single incident or the presence of a single victim. The story of Edward revealed the importance of looking at individual cases, for his experiences of bullying were institutionalized within the class. It appeared that he experienced little that was positive in his interactions with others and, even pupils who did not appear to pick on anyone else saw Edward as 'fair game'. However, in survey terms, he was but a single case.

If a school considers that to measure incidence levels of bullying is important then another issue to consider is the timing of any investigation. The dynamics of relationships in the class and staffs' understanding of them are not established until well into the school year and are subject to change throughout the year, therefore surveys should not be conducted at the beginning of the school year, but once relationship patterns have been established.

Contemporary interest and awareness means that pupils are prepared to talk openly about *the issue* of bullying, even if discussing their own involvement is not always easy. They are a repository of sophisticated thoughts and ideas and their involvement is paramount in generating ideas that counter any inertia that may exist, and therefore all types of post-event management developed that involve pupils are more likely to have a long-term impact.

Peer pressure groups influence, if not determine, relationships in the informal culture of the school and there is a need for a supportive 'audience' as part of the process of securing membership of the group. The significance of the peer group cannot be underestimated since the majority of episodes of bullying take place in the presence of peers and most of the remainder within the knowledge of peers. Salmivalli, Hutterton and Lagerspetz (1997) noted that between a third and half of incidents take place within a friendship network. The secrecy of bullying is not about keeping information from other pupils – they know about it – but is about not involving adults for fear that their action inflames the situation.

The informal culture of the school generates its own values and these may change with time. Amongst older pupils it is currently 'uncool' to be seen to work hard at school and to be a 'swot'. The challenge for educators is to make it as 'uncool' to be a bully as it is to be a 'swot', but this will not be easy, especially with the 8- to 14-year age group when the attitudes and values of pupils seem at their greatest distance from those of adults in schools. Children who have had no formal say in how bullying is dealt with in their school and who are dependent upon adults for solutions are both disempowered and distant. Only by being involved at every level can such pupils move beyond the passivity of their role and assume responsibility and more positive power. Edward, the case study, had looked to teachers for support and received little from his peers, as little was the expectation.

Open discourse between staff, pupils and parents on bullying can raise more questions than answers, but the value may have been in facilitating an understanding of the complexities of bullying, the similarities and dissimilarities of experience, and the attitudes that will lead to differential practice. Parents often perceive inertia prior to their intervention and it is often little more than a perception, resulting from the lack of a clear role for them. Just as there may be a fear within schools that developing policy on bullying alongside parents can be construed as admission that a school has a bullying problem, so, it seems, perpetuating exclusion of parents can serve to generate misunderstanding or ignorance. In this context the term 'parents' means all parents, not just those who visit their school when their child has been bullied or accused of being a bully.

Schools often suffer from imposed innovative fatigue and, as a consequence, moving towards the kinds of practices mentioned in this book constitutes a journey that may distract from fulfilling the requirements of externally enforced change. Yet schools have been *compelled* to develop policies on bullying and it forms part of the OFSTED inspection framework, complying with the proposition that 'if you don't do this, something unpleasant will happen to you'. It could well be that the development of anti-bullying strategies has been inhibited by such compulsion and that the time has come to reappraise how schools, and all the parties that contribute to their success, nurture and develop their own effective practice in countering bullying and how their experience can be shared with others. To finish here are the top ten pieces of advice in a preventative strategy.

The Top Ten Pieces of Advice in a Preventative Strategy

1 *Act early* because it shows that bullying is not acceptable in your class or school and it helps to prevent a single action turning into a relationship based on bullying.

2 Make sure that *all know the anti-bullying policy* (do not fall into the trap of calling it a 'bullying policy' – a mistake made by writers of policies and some books on the subject). Even better, make sure that as many pupils, parents, governors and staff as possible are involved in its creation. Ensure that preventative approaches are co-ordinated with approaches in the behaviour policy; better still, the 'whole-school positive relationships policy'. Above all revisit it regularly, remind yourself of its wisdom and write notes on it that will inform thinking when it is revised.

3 *Keep written records of observations, meetings and actions taken,* and make sure that records are kept in keeping with advice from your local authority. It is always helpful to develop a bullying report pro forma on which reported incidents are recorded and a pro forma for meetings with parents.

4 *Take bullying seriously as it is about the climate in which we learn.* Apart from the negative impact it has on all parties involved, it is likely to have a negative effect on learning.

5 *Hold awareness-raising workshops* with governors, parents and staff from other nearby 'feeder' schools. Do not be shy, celebrate the liberation of those who might live in fear of coming to and being in school.

6 *Become familiar with a variety of processes, strategies, skills and the philosophy that underpins them.* Behind an approach is a rationale that informs what it is trying to achieve. Failure to understand an approach can lead to negative comment, condemnatory attitudes and a dilution of its potential for change.

7 *Explore alternatives to punishment.* Punishment will not work for many of those who are punished regularly and can be counter-productive for the occasional minor misdemeanour. Exclusion from school because of bullying is a last resort and it is preferable, but not necessarily easy, to develop strategies involving adults and children that create a climate in which to bully would be anathema and in which it is dealt with effectively.

8 *Get away from the bully–victim model.* Powerful forces for change are bystanders and we are all bystanders. All members of the school community have a role to play in confronting negative relationships, helping bullies to change their behaviour and supporting victims.

9 *Gather information* through research – even better, help pupils to do this.

10 *Preventing bullying is about the school and classroom culture.* It is important that staff examine the school and themselves and consider the extent that bullying may be institutionalized rather than celebrating individuality, difference and the unusual, as a bullying culture thrives on ridiculing these features. We must not only tolerate difference but celebrate it and help children to make wise choices if they are to be active and responsible citizens.

Websites

This list is by no means comprehensive but does offer a breadth of websites. I have also included the intended focus, i.e. staff (S), children (C), parents (P).

Address	Focus
www.ace-ed.org.uk/bullying	P
www.education.unisa.edu.au/bullying	SCP
www.antibullying.net	SCP
www.bullystoppers.com	SCP
www.ofsted.gov.uk/publications/docs/3235.pdf	S
www.educate.co.uk/bullsug.htm	C
www.educationworld.com/a-tsl/archives/03-1/lesson002.shtml	S
www.thefieldfoundation.org	PS
www.parentcentre.gov.uk	P
www.scre.ac.uk/bully/	SP
www.kidscape.org.uk	SCP
www.parentlineplus.org.uk	P
www.dfes.gov.uk/bullying	SCP
www.bullying.co.uk	SCP
www.police.govt.nz/service/yes/nobully	CP
www.caper.com.au/	S
www.bullybeware.com/	SCP
www.bullyfreeworld.com	S
www.bbc.co.uk/schools/bullying	SCP
www.lfcc.on.ca/bully.htm	SP

Contacts

Anti-bullying Campaign	020 7378 1446
Advisory Centre for Education	020 7354 8321
The Children's Legal Centre	01206 873 820
Kidscape	020 7730 3300
Parentline plus	0808 800 2222

The following list is a selection of books that have proved useful as part of professional development courses and by staff working in schools. It is by no means exhaustive, but serves to illustrate the breadth of material available.

Beane, A. (1999) *The Bully Free Classroom*. Minneapolis, MIN: Free Spirit Publications.

Cowie H. and Wallace P. (2000) *Peer Support in Action*. London: Sage.

Donnellan, C. (2001) *Victims of Bullying*. Cambridge: Independence.

Elliott, M. and Kilpatrick, J. (1994) *How to Stop Bullying: A Kidscape Training Guide*. London: Kidscape.

Lines, D. (2002) *Brief Counselling in Schools: Working with Young People from 11 to 18*. London: Sage.

Rhodes, J. and Ajmal, Y. (1995) *Solution Focused Thinking in Schools*. London: BT Press.

Sullivan, K., Cleary, M. and Sullivan, G. (2004) *Bullying in Secondary Schools: What it Looks Like and How to Manage it*. London: Sage.

Stacey, H. and Robinson, P. (1997) *Let's Mediate*. Bristol: Lucky Duck.

Tyrrell, J. (2002) *Peer Mediation: A Process for Primary Schools*. London: Souvenir Press.

REFERENCES

Ahmad, Y., Whitney, I. and Smith, P. (1991) 'A survey for schools on bully/victim problems', in Smith, P. and Thompson, D. (eds) *Practical Approaches to Bullying*. London: David Fulton.

Askew, S. (1989) 'Aggressive behaviour in boys: to what extent is it institutionalised?' in Tattum, D. and Lane, D. (eds) *Bullying in Schools*. Stoke-on-Trent: Trentham Books.

Besag, V. (1989) *Bullies and Victims in Schools*. Buckingham: Open University Press.

Blatchford, P. (1996) 'Taking pupils seriously: recent research and initiatives on breaktime in schools', *Education 3–13*, 24 (3), pp. 60–5.

Blatchford, P. (1998) *Social Life in School: Pupils' Experience of Breaktime and Recess from 7–16 years*. London: Falmer Press.

Boulton, M. (1995) 'Playground behaviour and peer interaction patterns of primary school boys classified as bullies, victims and not involved', *British Journal of Educational Psychology*, 65, pp. 165–77.

Boulton, M. (1997) 'Teachers' views on bullying: definitions, attitudes and ability to cope', *British Journal of Educational Psychology*, 67 (2), pp. 223–33.

Bowers, L., Smith, P. and Binney, V. (1994) 'Perceived family relationships of bullies, victims and bully/victims in middle childhood', *Journal of Social and Personal Relationships*, 11, pp. 215–32.

Braithwaite, J. (1989) Crime, shame and reintegration. Cambridge: Cambridge University Press.

Brier, J. and Ahmad, Y. (1991) 'Developing a school court as a means of addressing bullying in schools', in Smith, P. and Thompson, D. (eds) *Practical Approaches to Bullying*. London: David Fulton.

Byrne, B. (1994) *Coping with Bullying in Schools*. London: Cassell.

Cartwright, N. (1996) 'Combating bullying in school: the role of peer helpers', in Cowie, H. and Sharp, S. (eds) *Peer Counselling in Schools: A Time to Listen*. London: David Fulton.

Casdagli, P. and Gobey, F. (1990) *'Only Playing, Miss!': the Playscript/Workshop In Schools*. Stoke-on-Trent: Trentham Books.

Clarkson, P. (1987) 'The bystander role', *Transactional Analysis Journal*, 17 (3), pp. 82–7.

Clarkson, P. (1996) *The Bystander (An End to Innocence in Human Relationships?)*. London: Whurr.

Cowie, H. (1995) 'Approaches to peer support: befriending, counselling and mediation', *Young Minds Newsletter*, 23 October.

Cowie, H. and Sharp, S. (1992) 'Students themselves tackle the problem of bullying', *Pastoral Care in Education*, 9 (4), pp. 31–7.

Cowie, H. and Wallace, P. (2000) *Peer Support in Action: From Bystanding to Standing By*. London: Sage.

Cowie, H., Boulton, M. and Smith, P. (1992) 'Bullying: pupil relationships', in Jones N. and Baglin-Jones E. (eds) *Learning to Behave: Curriculum Whole School Management Approaches to Discipline*. London: Kogan Page.

Cullingford, C. and Brown, G. (1995) 'Children's perceptions of victims and bullies', *Education 3-13*, 23 (2), pp. 11–16.

Department for Education (DfE) (1994) *Bullying: Don't Suffer in Silence: An Anti-bullying Pack for Schools*. London: HMSO.

Department for Education and Employment (DfEE) (1998) *Taking Forward our Plans to Raise Standards for All*. Sudbury: DfEE.

Department of Education and Science (DES) (1989) *Discipline in Schools – Report of the Committee of Enquiry: The Elton Report*. London: HMSO.

Elliott, M. (1997a) 'Bullies and victims', in Elliott, M. (ed.) *Bullying: A Practical Guide to Coping for Schools (2nd Edn)*. London: Pitman Publishing.

Elliott, M. (1997b) 'Bully courts', in Elliott, M. (ed.) *Bullying: A Practical Guide to Coping for Schools (2nd Edn)*. London: Pitman Publishing.

Eslea, M. and Smith, P. (1998) 'The long-term effectiveness of anti-bullying work in primary schools', *Educational Research*, 40 (2), pp. 203–18.

Hazler, R., Hoover, J. and Oliver, R. (1992) 'What kids say about bullying', *Executive Educator*, 14 (11), pp. 20–2.

Herbert, C. (1996) *Stop the Bullying*. Cambridge: Carrie Herbert Press.

Johnstone, M., Munn, P. and Edwards, L. (1992) *Action Against Bullying: A Support Pack for Schools*. Edinburgh: Scottish Council for Research in Education, the Scottish Office Education Department.

Knights, L. (1998) 'A student- and staff-developed anti-bullying initiative', *Pastoral Care in Education*, 16 (1), pp. 33–4.

La Fontaine, J. (1991) *Bullying: The Child's View*. London: Calouste Gulbenkian Foundation.

Lane, D. (1989) 'Bullying in school: the need for an integrated approach', *School Psychology International*, (10), pp. 211–15.

Laslett, R. (1982) 'A children's court for bullies', *Special Education: Forwards Trends*, 9 (1), pp. 9–11.

Lee, C. (1993) 'The perceptions of bullying in schools by pupils at the age of transition', *Collected Original Resources in Education*, 17 (3), Birmingham: Carfax.

Lee, C. (2001) 'Bullying in a primary school: a case study'. PhD dissertation, University of Plymouth.

Lines, D. (2002) *Brief Counselling in Schools: Working with Young People from 11 to 18*. London: Sage.

Lowenstein, L. (1978) 'Who is the bully?', *Bulletin of the British Psychological Society*, 31, pp 147–9.

Maines, B. and Robinson, G. (1991) 'Don't blame the bullies', *Educational Psychology in Practice*, 7 (3), pp. 168–72.

Maines, B. and Robinson, G. (1992) *The No-Blame Approach*. Bristol: Lame Duck.

Molnar, A. and Lindquist, B. (1990) *Changing Problem Behaviour in Schools*. San Francisco, CA: Jossey-Bass.

Office for Standards in Education (OFSTED) (2003) *Bullying: Effective Action in Secondary Schools*. Report HMI 465. London: The Stationery Office.

Oliver, C. and Candappa, M. (2003) *Tackling Bullying: Listening to the Views of Children and Young People*. London: Institute of Education/Department for Education and Skills.

Oliver, R., Young, T. and LaSalle S. (1994) 'Early lessons in bullying and victimization: the help and hindrance of children's literature', *School Counsellor*, 42, pp. 137–43.

Olweus, D. (1991) 'Bully/victim problems among schoolchildren: basic facts and effects of a school based intervention program', in Pepler, D. and Rubin, K. (eds) *The Development and Treatment of Childhood*. Hillsdale, NJ: Lawrence Erlbaum Associates.

Olweus, D. (1993) *Bullying in School: What We Know and What We Can Do*. Oxford: Blackwell.

Olweus, D. (1999) 'Sweden', in Smith, P., Motita, Y., Junger-Tas, J., Olweus, D., Catalano, R. and Slee, P. (eds) *The Nature of School Bullying: A Cross-National Perspective*. London: Routledge.

Pervin, K. (1995) 'Parental attitudes and beliefs about bullying: an investigation into parents whose children attend an inner-city school', *Pastoral Care and Education*, 13 (3), pp. 14–18.

Pervin, K. and Turner, A. (1994) 'An investigation into staff and pupils' knowledge, attitudes and beliefs about bullying in an inner-city school', *Pastoral Care and Education*, 12 (3), pp. 4–10.

Rigby, K. (1996) *Bullying in Schools and What to Do About It*. London: Jessica Kingsley.

Rigby, K. and Slee, P. (1991) 'Bullying among Australian school children: reported behaviour and attitudes toward victims', *Journal of Social Psychology*, 131 (5), pp. 615–27.

Salmivalli, C., Huttenton, A. and Lagerspetz, K. (1997) 'Peer networks and bullying in school', *Scandinavian Journal of Psychology*, 38, pp. 305–12.

Sharp, S. (1995) 'Self esteem, response style and victimisation: possible ways of preventing victimisation through parenting and school based training programmes'. Unpublished paper presented at ECER Conference, September, Bath.

Sharp, S. and Smith, P. (1994) *Tackling Bullying in Your School*. London: Routledge.

Sharp, S., Sellars, A. and Cowie, H. (1994) 'Time to listen: setting up a peer-counselling service to help tackle the problem of bullying in schools', *Pastoral Care in Education*, 12 (2), pp. 3–6.

Smith, P. (1991) 'The silent nightmare: bullying and victimisation in school peer groups', *Psychologist*, 4, pp. 243–8.

Stephenson, P. and Smith, D. (1987) 'Anatomy of a playground bully', *Education*, 18, pp. 236–7.

Stones, R. (ed.) (1998) *Children's Books about Bullying*. Reading: Books for Keeps.

Tattum, D. (1989) 'Bullying – a problem crying out for attention', *Pastoral Care in Education*, 7 (2), pp. 21–5.

Whitney, I. Nabuzoka, D. and Smith, P. (1992) 'Bullying in schools: mainstream and special needs', *Support for Learning*, 7 (1), pp. 3–7.

Whitney, I. and Smith, P. (1993) 'A survey of the nature and extent of bullying in junior/middle and secondary schools', *Educational Research*, 35 (1), pp. 3–25.

www.bullying.co.uk

www.dfes.gov.uk/bullying

Zehr, H. (1990) *Changing Lenses: a New Focus for Crime and Justice*. Scottdale, PA: Herald Press.

Zeigler, S. and Rosenstein-Manner, M. (1991) *Bullying at School: Toronto in an International Context*. Toronto: A report to the Toronto Board of Education, pp. 1–38.

INDEX